the
EASTERNERS'
guide to
WESTERN
Canada

the
EASTERNERS'
guide to
WESTERN
Canada

edited by
Ron Marken

Western Producer Prairie Books
Saskatoon, Saskatchewan

Humor: That quality which appeals to a sense of the ludicrous; something that is or is designed to be comical or amusing.

THE EASTERNERS' GUIDE TO WESTERN CANADA
Edited by Ron Marken

© 1985 Western Producer Prairie Books
Saskatoon, Saskatchewan

Cover and interior cartoons by Brian Gable
Cover design by Luba Zagurak
Photographs courtesy of: Government of Alberta, p. 36; Government of B.C., p. 50; *The Western Producer,* pp. 11 and 22; Sheila Bean, p. 12, no. 1, p. 63; All other photographs in the book by Ron Marken

Many thanks to Don and Betty Klepp, costumers.

Printed and bound in Canada by John Deyell Company

Western Producer Prairie Books publications are produced and manufactured in the middle of western Canada by a unique publishing venture owned by a group of prairie farmers who are members of the Saskatchewan Wheat Pool. From the first book in 1954, a reprint of a serial originally carried in the weekly newspaper, *The Western Producer,* to the book before you now, the tradition of providing enjoyable and informative reading for all Canadians is continued.

Canadian Cataloguing in Publication Data

Main entry under title:

The Easterners' guide to Western Canada

ISBN 0–88833–149–5

1. Canada, Western — Social life and customs — Anecdotes, facetiae, satire, etc.
2. Canadian wit and humor (English)*   3. Canadian wit and humor, Pictorial.   I. Marken, Ron, 1939–

FC173.E15 1985   971.064'7'0207   C85–091517–1
F1060.38.E15 1985

DEDICATION

ANOTHER ONE FOR PATRICIA.
She came from eastern Australia
And adopted western Canada
So she sees the funny side of everything.

ABOUT OUR AUTHORS

MARK ABLEY: Writes uncontrollably. *NOT* Mark Abley the bootlegger. From Montreal, more or less.

GAIL BOWEN: Once visited Vancouver. Read Jane Austen in her hotel room.

LORNA CROZIER: Not from Toronto. Sexier than she thinks, although voluntarily living in Regina.

MICHAEL GILLGANNON: A shepherd. Cable Address: flinflonman.

DON GILLMOR: Writing M.A. thesis on eastern Canada.

DON KERR: Hobby: Saving theatres. Ambition: To be a long-distance trucker. Not Right.

DON KLEPP: See "Naicam" in gazetteer. Occupation: Furs and Hides. Hobby: Barming.

PATRICK LANE: Has lived everywhere. Has done everything. Turn-offs? Insincere people.

ROD MCINTYRE: Witty, spirited, and compassionate. One of three Westerners who has seen Prince Edward Island.

RON MARKEN: Manitoba coal-heaver. Recently arrested for frequentage; all charges dropped.

GRINDLEY MATTHEWS: Consultant in neo-adolescent interior design.

HILDY RHODES: Ex-Minister of Manpower in a Federal Liberal Government. From Toronto. No other qualifications.

LAIRD STEVENS: Fled Manitoba in 1981; Manitoba in hot pursuit. Address withheld.

GERTRUDE STORY: Human being, now in private practice. Makes house calls in Prince Albert.

WILLY THOMAS: Big. Plays Center for the Saskatchewan Roughriders.

TABLE of CONTENTS

SO YOU WANT TO KNOW MORE ABOUT THE WEST

In western Canada, the natives may be restless, but they are still friendly. For the time being. (Except for several Indians, Métis, farmers, women, pensioners, Japanese, students, oilmen, workers, artists, mothers, and both Liberals.) Therefore, it is always best to understand your quarry. Don't blunder. Know enough to stand downwind of a fox and upwind of a skunk.

Don't stride into the Westerner's wide open space, saying, "Hi there. I'm from Toronto. Love me!" Some pockets of Canadians still devoutly wish Toronto would fly to Lichtenstein and join the European Economic Community. These pockets are roughly the size of Manitoba, Saskatchewan, Alberta, and British Columbia. Watch for them.

In grade three, you scorned American ignorance of Canada. Remember how insulted you were when they laughed at your "play money"? They had never heard of Lester Pearson! They thought the Montreal Alouettes were an all-girl rock group!

Westerners feel *doubly* insulted: Americans think they are Montana. Eastern Canadians think the Kicking Horse Pass is a Yonge Street bar. Eastern ignorance of the Great Canadian West is monumental.

But that benightedness will be dissolved. We offer here what "professional educators" call "SKILLS":
Skills to return alive from the DARKEST KOOTENAYS!
Skills to endure the awful terrors of DUCK MOUNTAIN!
Skills to survive the jeopardies of THE MIGHTY PEACE!

Welcome to the wonderful world of the West! Cast aside your robes of ignorance! Foreswear forever your narrowmindedness! What you are about to read will surpass the repatriated Constitution in its power to unite Canadians. Indeed, we will find that there is much more binding this country together than just Canadian Tire.

Ron Marken

NOT YOUR AVERAGE TRAVEL GUIDE

by Mark Abley

Tourists are welcome in the West. Last year, both visitors had the time of their lives. It's a shame that most Easterners stay away.

But who can blame them? The West has an outdated, misleading image. Pick up the standard travel guide — *Fodor's Canada* — and you'll find that the province of Alberta writhes below the heading "Land of the Fearsome Blackfoot"; Manitoba, meanwhile, tosses and turns under the label "Home of the Hudson's Bay Co." It's as if no self-respecting Haligonian could possibly visit Winnipeg without trading in some pelts for a blanket. The blanket would keep him warm on his journey through the wilds of Saskatchewan, "The Land of Outdoor Fun."

Travellers need help — real help. Easterners with a few weeks to spare could use guidance in comprehending the folkways of the West, interpreting the native dialect. If you thirst for worthy useless knowledge ("Canada's only known natural supply of sodium sulfate is located here"), buy a copy of *Fodor's*. For practical assistance, read on.

YOU GOTTA BE TOUGH TO LIVE HERE

by Lorna Crozier

How can you identify a prairie male at a singles' party? He's not the one who saunters up and says, "Hi, I'm a Libra. What sign are you?" He's not the one who asks if you like hot tubs, or if you're a vegetarian. He's the one who makes his move just as you're at the door, pulling on your mitts, winding your green and white scarf around your neck. He clears his throat, pauses, and asks: "Is it cold enough for you?"

Prairie people love it when it's cold. A Westerner's idea of a good time is to plunk you in front of the TV and watch your face when the weatherman warns, "Exposed flesh will freeze in less than a minute." Understandably so. In the days before indoor plumbing, you had to dash from the back door to the outhouse, expose only the necessary amount of flesh, then high tail it back, all in under a minute.

The prairie obsession with weather doesn't end when spring begins. Just after they plant the delicate tomatoes they've nurtured under a growing light, clouds crash the garden party and dump three inches of snow on the green shoots, the chaise longue, and the steaks sizzling on the barbecue they hauled out of the basement in a moment of wild optimism. After all, it is the end of May.

The weather is talked about most when it is the best. On beautiful July and August afternoons when the mercury climbs as high as a cat up a poplar, and everyone, covered in coconut and palm oil, smells good enough to eat. Finally, they can lie back in a Mexican hammock, a Boh in one hand, mosquito repellent in the other, and enjoy. But no. Now you have to feel guilty. Guilty! Because if the day is gorgeous, if the weather couldn't be better in the trailer courts of Phoenix or on the beaches of Miami, that means it isn't raining. And if it isn't raining, what about the farmers? While you're lying in the sun, some poor farmer is watching his land blow all the way to Sault Ste. Marie.

Even if you've lived here all your life, if you're under 65, you haven't experienced *real* cold, *real* wind, *real* drought. "Why, you should have been around when the cyclone hit Regina in 1912 and carried the naked woman in her bathtub right out her window into the sky like Winken, Blinken and Nod and set her down in the middle of Victoria Avenue."

"You should have been here in 1916 when the wind was so strong, the grass so dry, a match lit in one town started a fire hundreds of miles away."

"Or the fall of '22. I've never seen anything like it. It was so cold the chickens decided to migrate and we had to drive all the way to North Dakota to pick them up. That same year, the flame in the coal oil lantern froze while I was doing chores. And our voices, I'm telling you, they froze between the house and the barn, and in the spring when they melted, you wouldn't believe the racket."

"But '37 was the worst. So much farm land in the sky, you couldn't see the nose on your face. That was the year they shut down the sports day. During our final game, my brother Fred got lost between second and third when he tried to steal a base, and we haven't seen him since."

Let's face it. There's more weather here than in any other part of the country. There's so much weather, it's all they can talk about. "Is it cold enough for you?" You bet.

YA HEARD ABOUT THAT DEPRESSION?

by Don Kerr

You can't know the West unless you know the Depression and the way to know the Depression these days is to interview the survivors, only they've been interviewed so often lately some of them are suffering from tape recorder burn. A student goes out to interview two old coots in a town that looks like a broken fence that hasn't been painted since the year when the farmers didn't complain.

Student: Hello, I wonder if I could talk to you about the Depression.
Ben: Yep.
Burt: Yep.
Student: Well, uh, I heard there were a lot of grasshoppers back then.
Burt: Yep.
Ben: Yep.
Student: Like, were there many?
Burt: Yep.
Ben: Yep.
Student: They, uh, do any damage?
Burt: Ate the crop.
Ben: Just like the family.
Student: Pardon?
Ben: Invited themselves for dinner.
Burt: More like your family.
Ben: Yep.
Student: They were bad then?
Ben: Yep.

Burt: You leave a jacket in the field, come back next day, it was gone.
Student: They'd eaten it?
Burt: Yep.
Ben: Or hopped off with it.
Burt: Ate the handles off forks.
Student: Yeah?
Burt: Where the sweat was, salty, they liked salt.
Ben: Liked anything. Eat anything.
Burt: Yep.
Ben: Yep. Ate . . . who was it now? Johanssons, that's it, ate their farmhouse. Went away for a weekend at the lake. Came back. All gone. And them grasshoppers picking their teeth.
Burt: Times was tough for grasshoppers too you know. Wasn't a heck of a lot around here for anyone to eat.
Ben: Yep.
Burt: Ate two towns on the Willowbunch line.
Ben: Folks all gone to a ball tournament.
Burt: What were the names of them towns?
Ben: Porkhock and Kidney.
Burt: Yep.
Student: Oh, sure.
Ben: Or was it Beansprout?
Burt: Yep.
Ben: Ate everything.
Burt: Used to attack the chickens but they'd met their match there.
Ben: Yep. A chicken is as mean as a grasshopper.
Burt: Yep.
Ben: Yep.
Burt: Ate children.
Student: What?
Burt: O'Kellys lost six kids to the grasshoppers.
Student: Ah, cut it out.
Burt: Yep. Grasshoppers ate the crop. Old O'Kelly hit the rails to work in B.C. Left his wife at home.
Ben: Gone for six years.
Burt: Well, you see for the O'Kellys that was six kids.
Ben: Yep. Lost six kids to the grasshoppers.

THE LAND
by Rod McIntyre

What is in the West? There are only two things — The Land and The Sky. Let me dwell on The Land.

We are Of The Land. It takes the eye of a Westerner to see its beauty, — an eye filled with dust. Put all that dust together and you have The Land. Take away The Land and you have nothing. For it is The Land that grows things. The West without dust would be a bleak and terrible place. Worse than two thousand miles of precambrian rock with festering cities filling rivers and lakes with acid and lead. A veritable rhyme for hell.

Here the fertile land grows a variety of things that are only stunted and misshapen in other parts of Canada. What does our garden grow? The western garden grows wheat and weeds.

Let me cultivate weeds. Of our five cultivatable noxious western weeds, two do well in snow and one on ice. The other two apparently drift with the prevailing wind. The two that do well in snow are the repottable *Conservatus insidius* and the perennial *Liberala gritae*, which grows in circles. The variety that thrives on ice is the *creeping Socialis hordis*. The *western dementia conceptus* and the *Socialis crassula*, both psychotic succulents, leech off the right side of the *Conservatus insidius*.

The *Conservatus insidius* has been seen in almost every province in the Dominion and carries with it a little known fungus that causes the spread of capitalism. Plant *Conservatus insidius* in a dark place like a vault, where its little roots will grow in perverse proportion to the shrinking dollar. The *Liberala gritae*, on the other hand, is growing increasingly rare in the West.

This *creeping Socialis hordis* thrives on ice.

Still, it performs a useful function in breaking wind from the East. Please report any citings to the "Hark! Lalonde Mall of Flame" in Calgary.

The *Socialis crassula* loathes blossoms. It also loathes sunshine, snow, and the CBC — in fact, everything but itself. Keep your *crassula* very wet and feed it teachers. (If teachers are scarce, loggers will do.)

The *western dementia conceptus* grows fitfully across western Canada. To encourage development of its identifying characteristic, the roseate neck, sing "O Canada" to it in French.

Put your *creeping Socialis hordis* in the basement under the furnace. It prefers to start on the bottom and work its way up. Never plant a *hordis* alone. It likes to form committees and grow by consensus.

Like all varieties, these noxious cultivatables have subspecies. From the *Liberala gritae* family comes the *Russet Thatchwort*. This plant does extremely well in cowboy boots and snow. Recent attempts to root the Blue-Eyed-Where-Have-You-Bean (which thrives in manure from white chargers) in Vancouver have met with modest success, but only where it was planted in the shade of the Flowering Handsome, sometimes called the *lona campaignalis*.

From the *Conservatus insidius* family come three notable subspecies: the Devine Gloryblower, the Staring Lyons, and the Lougheed-of-the-Night. All three of these plants do well when supported by polls. The Devine Gloryblower is a remarkable plant that thinks it's God. The Staring Lyons is now rare, strangled by a local infestation of *creeping Socialis hordis*. The Lougheed-of-the-Night likes old football helmets and steeps its roots in heavy oil. It is, perhaps, the most vigorous of the *Conservatus* subspecies, though no longer in full bloom.

Although the *western dementia conceptus* is a good natural laxative, it appears to be sterile; however, airborne spores from the *Collvera Richardus* subspecies (copious in Colorado and Arizona) appear to cause irregularity — if eaten in courtrooms.

The *western dementia conceptus* in full bloom.

Two remarkable specimens of the *Socialis crassula* deserve note. The Earnest Mandrake grows tastefully if denied distilled spirits and exposed to elementary Gospel music. Its leaves are considered medicinal, but should only be taken eternally. The Whacking Beenut, on the other hand, dances to its own music and makes deals you can't refuse. (For their own good, keep other plants away from the Whacking Beenut; however, they might find the company of the Earnest Mandrake consoling — until they find that it refuses them all pleasures.)

Finally we have the *creeping Socialis hordis*. The populist subspecies are the Blakegrass and the Pawleaf Flytrap varieties. The Pawleaf Flytrap is one of the more successful *hordis* subspecies. Both have fragile grass roots and have been observed bedding with *Liberala gritae*. Occasionally they do well on their own, especially when grown on the left side of the road — either against the traffic or under it. They are both edible and make excellent roughage in the naturally gritty "Worker-Farmer Salad."

All these things are visible to the wrinkle-wreathed, silent, squint-eye of the Westerner, because the Westerner is of The Land. Only when the Easterner drinks of the cup of Western Water (i.e., Regina water — which is The Land in liquid form) will this stunning array of noxious cultivatables be made visible to the eastern eye.

Aide to John Turner observes phenomenal growth of *Conservatus insidius* in western Canada.

THE SEVEN WONDERS OF THE WEST

1. The Climax Hotel, Saskatchewan. Honeymoon capital of the known world.

2. The Rites of Spring

3. The West Edmonton Mall.

4. Last Mountain Ski Resort and Slalom Run, with tow ropes and lift.

5. The eleventh hole, Flin Flon Country Club, Manitoba.

6. The B.C. Liberal public trough: a last gesture by outgoing PM, P.E. Trudeau.

7. Calgary's Saddle Dome.

HOW TO TELL THE PEOPLE OF THE PLAINS
by Gertrude Story

No Easterner would be caught dead in the prairie West except at his touring mother's unexpected funeral. And only then if she refuses — silent and accusing in her coffin — to suffer her body to traverse those drab and godforsaken Canada Number 1 plains once more, even to be decently interred in Etobicoke or Charlottetown.

A Westerner appreciates an Easterner's dislike of the prairies — especially if the Westerner has just come in the house for dinner after counting newly hatched grasshoppers.

If you don't like the West, intimates the Westerner, then don't bother to come out here, 'cause if you do, we'll just lose all respect for your judgment.

And after the Westerner's complained about the high price of car fuel and the high price of government; after he's cussed the early grasshoppers, the late spring, and the heat and the cold and God, you ask him why he stays here. And he says, "Where else would I go?" *That's* a Westerner.

You can tell a Westerner by the way they've got myopia. You can always tell a Westerner by the way he feels obliged to live up to his CBC image. And you can always tell a Westerner by his scientific beefalos. And that's a fact.

You're at a prairie gas pump. The guy at the pumps pulls his John Deere hat over his eyebrows, squints into the sun, cusses God, the grasshoppers, and asks "Fill 'er up?"

"I'll take two dollars worth," you say.

"Oh, from the East I see," he says. "Figure there's a pump at the next corner, eh? Wal, I guess I'll just fill 'er up for you. There ain't even a *corner* at the next corner for the next two hundred miles."

So you stand there watching the flitter-fluttery dove on your brand new Royal Bank Visa taking off into the sun on wings of lyrical petrol-fume. "Watch out for the beefalo!" bellows the gas jock. You duck. He laughs. "Watch out for the beefalo. Just down the road," he says. "Right hand side. Beefalo. Tony Miner's farm. Five hundred of 'em. Part beef cow, part buffalo."

"Scientific," he says, listening, ear cocked, for the nearly-full gurgle in your gas tank before carefully spilling ninety cents worth into the dust to discourage the grasshoppers. "That's what Tony Miner says," he says. "It's all done scientific."

You can always tell a Westerner by the way he explains everything, whether you want to hear it or not.

"You know how wide the arse end of a cow is, eh?" he says. "And you know how wide is the hump on the front end of them buffalo, eh?"

"Wal-sir," he says, "They've took the arse end of a cow and matched her, scientific, with the hump end of a buffalo. And if that don't give you beefalo burgers enough for the Summer Days Rodeo outa one carcass, why, there's something funny."

"Scientific," he repeats. "They do it scientific." A Westerner loves that.

No matter how lurid an idea is — from a cow that isn't a cow to a trust company that can't be trusted — if you tell a Westerner it's scientific, he'll eat it or put his money into it and love the whole of it inside a minute.

AMAZE YOUR FRIENDS!
COMB PLAYING WESTERN STYLE
Don Klepp

This instruction manual features the Buxton Mouthcomb Songster favoured by Humphry and the Dumptrucks jug band, the Doukhobor Nude Street Theatre Ensemble, and the Grouse Mountain Ski Patrol Mouthcomb Quintet.

The Songster is the generic term for a mouthcomb, just as Kleenex has become the generic term for facial tissue.

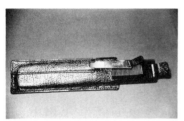

Figure 1.
The Buxton No. 66 Gift Set.

The instrument's construction is transparently simple: a diaphragm stretched over a comb body. The comb body is part of the Buxton No. 66 gift set: a comb, nail file, and leather carrying case (Fig. 1). "66" means that the comb has 66 teeth. More important, this means that the comb body has 67 spaces, which gives the Songster a total range of three and a half octaves.

The shank, arms, and teeth of the comb body (Fig. 2) are high-density, polystrenic plastic with a tensile strength of 15 kg/cm. This means an adult male can easily bend the comb's shank (Fig. 3). (Bending produces the rapidly tongued quarter-notes made famous by the comb quintet of the Grouse Mountain Ski Patrol Mouthcomb Quintet.) With the pressure released, the shank returns snappily to its flat profile for conventional playing.

Figure 2.
The Mouthcomb Body.

At the grip end of the shank there is a thong of No. 24 cowhide with two functions: it allows the comb to be easily pulled from its case and it allows the instrument to be firmly gripped during spirited playing.

The player holds a diaphragm over the comb body (Fig. 3). The distinctive music is regulated by the 0.068 cm spacing between the teeth; this spacing allows limited inter-tooth diaphragm travel and produces a sound half an octave higher than the initiating hum.

Figure 3.
Diaphragm Stretched Over
Comb Body.

Figure 4.
Detail of the Wrinkle Factor of Diaphragm (x3).

Figure 5.
Using the File to do the Preliminary Tuning.

Traditionally, the diaphragm is made from the wrapper of a two-ply, 15-tissue, Kleenex Pocket-Pack. To reach the highest standards, this pack must be carried in the pocket of an active person for at least five days. These conditions create a wrinkle factor (Fig. 4) of 16 microgons and a stretch range of 1.5% to 3.5%.

When the seasoned Kleenex pack is emptied, the end walls of the package are slit to spread out the wrapper. The resultant diaphragm has two main playing surfaces, one above and one below the laminated double thickness which forms an "I" in the centre of the wrapper. (The centre "I" is too thick to produce a good sound.)

In operation, the Songster takes its distinctive tone from the pursing of the player's lips against the tightly stretched diaphragm. The Songster must be tuned each time it is played. Indeed, the tuning usually proves to be a most difficult chore for the beginner. First, the Songster must be carefully cleaned and evenly spaced (Fig. 5). Then lips, diaphragm, and comb body must be finely adjusted to achieve the right tone.

The "right" tone varies from player to player. However, a good player is always brassy. The slide notes of a trombone can be evoked on the well-played Songster. There is often a hint of the brassy quarter-note exuberance characterizing Louis Armstrong's early coronet playing. The quarter notes are produced by double-tonguing, known properly as *duolingus* and colloquially as "French playing."

Figure 6a.

Figure 6b.

Figure 6c.

Figure 6a shows the proper thumb position on the grip thong. The effect is relaxed, never desperate or clutching. Figure 6b illustrates finger positioning for "free playing," which produces a smooth sound with minimal finger obstruction. In Figure 6c the player is concentrating on the double fingering, a necessary part of the technique used to play staccato quarter notes in *duolingus* playing.

Mouthcomb music is now available on tape. In 1983, the CBC broadcast "The Hans Selyestrom Series," in memory of the Grouse Mountain ski patroller who perished in the avalanche he triggered playing his Buxton Songster in April, 1975.

The Grouse Mountain Ski Patrol

FOLK HEROES
OF WESTERN CANADA
(Does Not Include Wayne Gretzky)

EMILY CARR: Unknown B.C. painter. Began imitating the Group of Seven, the only artistic style understood by Torontonians, who then pronounced her "famous."

CHIEF DAN GEORGE: Successfully demonstrated that there is life after retirement. Met Hollywood definition of stereotypical North American Indian.

MARGARET LAURENCE: Equal opportunity employer of 15,296 Ontario censors.

LOUIS RIEL: An insane and vicious murderer who led a cult-type insurrection in Manitoba and fled to the United States.

THE CROW: Unseen and legendary bird. Adored with worshipful ardour. Outlawed by Evil Quebecer, J.L. Pepin.

LOUIS RIEL: A prairie statesman who helped achieve effective self-government in Manitoba and prevented U.S. annexation.

TOMMY DOUGLAS: Launched North America's first socialist government (caused Ronald Reagan to turn over in his makeup). Left before that government started breaking strikes and selling uranium to whoever had the money. Living symbol of prairie pragmatism and self-righteousness.

KEITH MORRISON: TV news anchorman and graduate of the Canadian National Institute for the Bland but incredibly good-looking.

DIANE JONES KONIHOWSKI: Could lift Pat Marsden. More articulate than Johnny Esaw. Better looking than Keith Morrison. Able to leap tall buildings at a single bound.

W.O. MITCHELL: Defined prairie farm life for all Canadians studying Grade IX literature. A "family" author whose vocabulary of cuss words runs into the millions, Mitchell best summed up the Westerner: "Pest-proud."

NANCY GREENE RAINE: Forerunner of Steve Podborski. Now sells chair lifts and chocolate bars.

LOUIS RIEL: A lunatic Saskatchewan rebel who denied Gabriel Dumont adequate logistical support and tactical flexibility in Dumont's campaign for truth, justice, and the Crowsnest Pass Grain Freight Rates.

KAREN MAGNUSSON: World-class athlete who did not use her fame to promote feminine sanitary products.

JOE CLARK: Unable to leap tall buildings at a single bound. As articulate as Johnny Esaw. Might touch his Adam's apple with his chin and stop speaking forever. Will then be made senator within fifteen minutes.

LOUIS RIEL: Duly elected member of Parliament who was denied his seat in the Commons by the Eastern establishment.

VALDY: Aging singer. Grows alfalfa sprouts. Eats kelp. Has cut records.

DAVID STEINBERG: The first and last funny person to come out of Winnipeg. c.f., Sterling Lyon, Howard Pawley.

GORDIE HOWE: Until age fifty, earned his living hitting teenagers.

ALLAN FOTHERINGHAM: Almost a Moose Jaw boy, moved to *Maclean's* in order to skewer the Ottawa establishment and be near Anna Porter. Currently contesting one thousand nine hundred and eighty-five libel charges by eastern bigwigs. There is no higher western accolade.

CHARLIE FARQUHARSON: Got yer stereophonic farmer image there and turned it into somethin' Easterners could laugh at. Easterners are easily amused.

BOBBY GIMBY: On the day of Canada's centennial, set the indigenous music industry back one hundred years.

THE BRONFMANS: Tested a stringent potion on the citizens of Yorkton, Sask. Took it to Montreal, bottled it, and made millions.

RON LANCASTER: Realized in 1981 that brush cuts were no longer "in." Immediately hired by the CBC. Known in media circles as the "Little Generalizer."

BRUNO GERUSSI: Has successfully conquered the East on stage, on radio, and on television. Can break solid hollow core plywood with his bare hands.

CANADIAN GOTHIC

A MEDICINAL TIP
by Mark Abley

Tourists on the prairies may be puzzled by the many references to "sloughs." A slough is not a stagnant pool of water; the word for that is "pond." A slough is a prairie term for a "severe, loud cough." The question, "Got any ducks nesting on your slough?" means "Do you have the misfortune to suffer from a sore throat as well as a severe, loud cough?" Go into any drugstore between Banff and Lake of the Woods; and ask for a bottle of slough medicine. The strongest potion comes in a medicine hat.

PROVINCIAL FRONTIERS

The Manitoba Frontier. Wildlife patrolled.

Customs and Immigration
Saskatchewan.

The Alberta Frontier. Go heavily armed.

The B.C. Frontier. Keeping out the creeping
Socialis hordis.

FROM FURROW TO FREEWAY
HOW TO DRIVE
ON THE PRAIRIES AND LIVE!
by Ron Marken

In the last eighteen months, three drivers from Montreal — legendary for its sadistic driving — have immigrated to the West — one to Brandon, one to Prince Albert, one to Lacombe. All three are in their early thirties. In less than two short years, one has gone bald and the other two are prematurely white. Excellent drivers, each found driving on the prairies to be complicated; pathologically complicated.

Drivers from Thunder Bay will note the illusion of utter emptiness — fostered by an unlimited horizontal horizon. *Dangerous thinking!* People who think they are alone drive funny.

Open spaces and agriculture have made our driver oblivious to the traffic lane. In the field, he straddles the furrows with the wheels of his tractor and, at the end of a ploughed row, he makes a beautiful sweeping turn to head back for another pass at the sod. Put this driver in a car on a street, and the results are plain to anyone in Calgary, Estevan, or St. Boniface.

Making a right turn, he mimes his tractor at the end of the furrow, giving the steering wheel a swing to the *left* just before curling *right*. This is the famed *loopleft-curlright.*

A lively variation on the Loopleft-Curlright is the *omigod-loopleft-curlright-outofcentrelane!* You can do this without raising eyebrows in

Camrose, Alberta, but drivers from other parts of the world find such turns disconcerting.

Driver education on the prairies

This person was taught driving by a time-honoured procedure, ritual in its purity. At twelve years, he establishes driving habits making unsupervised forays through fields, back roads, herds of cattle, and chicken coops driving a tractor, an over-powered snowmobile, and the farm's half-ton, always at full throttle and never with a muffler. Then, before he's permanently licensed for life, his father guides him through the FOUR RULES OF THE PRAIRIE ROAD:

RULE ONE: "That's the brake. That's the footfeed. Step on one when yer goin' inta town. Step on t'other when yer there. It's easy."

Strangers will know they have crossed the shadow line between East and West when they notice that no car ever stops at a Stop sign. Sissies stop. Slow down for a Yield sign? Your girl-friend will never wear your curling jacket again.

RULE TWO: "Them road signs're only for people from outa province. Ignore 'em."

This dictum makes invisible such boring injunctions as "Slow School" or "Pedestrian Crosswalk" and "50 kpm Max" or "Slippery When Wet."

Only one sign attracts any notice: "Buckle Your Seat Belt, It's the Law." "Seatbelts are an imposition on my personal freedom, same as wearing a skidoo helmet. No goddam gov'ment can make me put one a them death-straps around *my* body!"

RULE THREE: "A yellow light means 'Floor it!' "

Recently, this high-spirited practice has evolved into a more sophisticated maxim: "A light that ain't bin red very long means 'Floor it !' "

This subtle interpretation of the international symbolism of red-amber-green causes visitors to remark on the anxiety etched onto the faces of western pedestrians. They are ready to jump to safety — always.

RULE FOUR: "Only faggots signal."

Only spinster grade two teachers make turning signals. *Real* prairie drivers use signal lights to annoy other patrons at drive-in theatres.

If you remember the FOUR RULES you too can drive through Moose Jaw and live.

Postscript
Going through the small towns along your holiday way, *do not relax.* Little villages, seemingly quiet, half-tons innocently nuzzling the hotel, main streets eddying in lazy summer dust: these hamlets are the breeding grounds for 83 percent of all western drivers. You are looking at The Source.

Respectfully admire this awesome fecundity, stranger. Then move on. Quietly. You'll be just fine — probably — until you get to the mountains.

READING WESTERN ROAD SIGNS

What Do These Signs Mean?:

 Last gas for 300 miles. Diesel only.

 Thick coffee. Stand a spoon upright in it.

 At night one person must always keep watch for tornadoes.

 "This sign sponsored by Cut Knife Tent and Awning Mfg. Co. Have a Nice Day."

 Locals customarily store farm implements in the living room.

 Enjoy your holiday. But never throw your frisbee too hard.

 This sign painted by the great Albrecht Durer's great-great-great-great-niece's great grandson.

 After putting the manure-spreader in the living room, draw the wagons into a circle.

 Hay for sale in selected outlets.

 Whiskbroom Capital of Canada.

If you cannot draw your wagons into a circle, put them on top of the car.

Lights out at 10.00 p.m. Blackout in effect.

MANITOBA MYSTIQUE
IT AIN'T EXACTLY
A FAMOUS PARFUM
by Laird Stevens

"It's a slice," you mutter miserably into your Seven-Eleven coffee. Only two weeks ago you were a happy eastern liberal whose every spare moment was spent growing trendy bonsai daisies that thrived on a subtle blend of Keith Jarret and light classics. You held romantic views on the role women and other less necessary minorities should be assuming in the all-new constitutionalized version of the Great White North. Life was bouncy and fresh.

Then you were unexpectedly transferred to Winnipeg, and the known world more or less flew out the window. People started telling you to "Go for it," without in the least specifying what manner of thing you were meant to have gone for. Moreover, certain things were inexplicably referred to as "slices." "What in God's name," you mumble morosely into your donut, "is a slice?"

Well, a slice is simply part of the Manitoba mystique. If you haven't managed *slice* after two weeks, you need help. Before you arrived, you thought of Manitoba simply as the rectangular province on the right of the other rectangular provinces in the atlas. This thumbnail sketch will no longer do. You're *here* now. Your western horizon needs fleshing out.

Not for nothing is the first town in Manitoba west of the Ontario border called Waugh. "Waugh" is a characteristically Eastern response to the "Welcome to Manitoba" signs on the border. (The town used to be called Waaaauuugggh, but the name was shortened when it wouldn't fit on the sign.)

If you love routine, you'll love Winnipeg. First, you'll have to go to work at the Wheat Board. Winnipeg works at the Wheat Board. That's why the transit system is set up the way it is. Wherever in the city you catch a bus, it will go to Portage and Main, right outside the Wheat Board. This ritualized existence is so hypnotic that it is common to see hordes of Winnipeggers hanging around outside the Wheat Board on a Saturday morning, wondering what to do with themselves.

Some of them eat. Eating is easy because you don't need a menu. Winnipeggers do not enjoy a varied cuisine. You will be pretty lucky to get peas and carrots, let alone anything exotic like broccoli. Usually, you will eat surf 'n' turf with a dose of salad bar. Surf 'n' turf consists of lobster and beef, cleverly cooked to taste exactly alike. However, you will get at least a pound of each along with an enormous baked potato and a soup bowl full of bacon bits. Don't expect to find anything remotely gay in the salad — like endives or artichokes; it is mostly celery and radishes and Thousand Island dressing. An unwritten rule in Winnipeg lets you substitute pizza for surf 'n' turf on Fridays.

What the citizenry themselves say about Winnipeg is instructive. They say it "has miles and miles . . . of miles." This not only describes Winnipeg to a T, but also the calibre of wit you are likely to encounter.

Moving around is also easy; there are only two places in Manitoba: Winnipeg and everywhere else. And Winnipeg is really the only place you want to be.

When you first arrived, you may not have equated Winnipeg with Mecca, the Garden of Eden, or anywhere where life is generally reputed to be a dish decked out entirely in maraschinos. A quick casting of the eye around the rest of Manitoba, however, will do much to help you revise this opinion.

Take Winnipegosis, for instance. This is not a disease that seeps at you through the ventilation system at the Wheat Board; it is a town. Other towns are equally evocative: East Braintree is my favourite.

Close-up of Manitoba.

It's no accident that the TransCanada Highway disdains everything between Winnipeg and Regina (with the doubtful exception of Brandon). Its course wasn't plotted by aliens who thought it might be fun to channel tourists through Swan River and The Pas, where it is more or less the custom to welcome outsiders with a momentary glower and a swift jab to the nose. No, it was mapped by Winnipeggers who know — or have heard tell — of the hairy hordes beyond their walls and who have done their best to steer the highway around all potential disaster areas.

Learn to say, "Win Win Winnipeg." It can't be any harder than "Ontari-ari-ari-o" or "Kaybec."

"PARLEZ-VOUS CALGARIE?"
THE LANGUAGE OF LOVE REVISITED
by Don Gillmor

In grade seven at John Diefenbaker Junior High, Calgary, my classmates would have taken gunshot wounds over French instruction. But there we were in Conversational French 10, waiting for our teacher. We assumed she would be a nineteen-year-old French actress. A common notion held that France was populated entirely by nineteen-year-old actresses and resistance types in berets. Our teacher, Madame St. Yves, arrived, defining a third category: short middle-aged women who looked like Ernest Borgnine.

Writing her name on the blackboard she announced, "French is the language of love."

"If I'm desperate and you're lucky," replied Robert Plosky, earning himself a week of detention and a permanent seat in the Unilingual Hall of Fame.

Madame St. Yves's initial aim, to have us all reading *Les Misérables* by the end of grade nine, was soon altered. We learned to count to fifty and to introduce ourselves successfully to some mythical "Madame Thibault."

High school triggered hormone explosions in the student body, leaving us with pimples on our backs and one thing on our minds. Under ideal conditions, learning French is not easy, especially having to ascribe a gender to everything. Into this maelstrom of glandular longing came our new French teacher, Mrs. Monson.

She was of the nineteen-year-old actress persuasion and her short skirts and fluent walk suggested many French things to our febrile minds. But after three years of study, with a well-documented facility for counting and an ability to identify *poulet* as chicken, we reached high school. The romance had been taken out of this alleged romance language . . . and much of the language as well.

The notion that we lived in a bilingual country was accorded the same credibility as UFO sightings by cattle ranchers. We didn't think one would ever land in our city.

Throughout high school, our knowledge of French Canadian culture developed from two sources: our French textbook and Tim Garneau, a classmate claiming a Quebec birthplace (later revealed to be Weyburn, Saskatchewan). Tim informed us that French Canadian girls had sexual erudition magically descend on them in adolescence. Born with the ability to sustain a French kiss indefinitely, they believed that sex was healthy. *I* didn't believe that sex was healthy, though I had yet to widen my circle of partners beyond myself. Perhaps it got healthier as you included other people? That seemed to contradict our recent guidance film, *A Minute of Pleasure, a Lifetime of Guilt.* According to Tim, the last word on Quebec was that the men played hockey and made bombs, and the women dreamed about sex all day.

We immediately spotted incongruities between Tim's testimonials and the photographs in our text, *Images de la France.* Gallic sexual verve was well hidden in the decidedly unhip duo of "Lucienne et Marie." Marie looked like she had one foot in the convent. Their constant companions, "Georges et François," with their brush cuts and dark suits, looked like candidates for an FBI training program in Salt Lake City. Their endless rendezvous' produced only a number of *sportif* costume changes and conversations that relied a little too heavily on the whereabouts of Madelaine for their sparkle. The France we had imagined — beautiful women, exciting rendezvous', romance — was belied by the photographs of Marie teasing her beehive and reciting her lunch menu. We concluded that French Canada was similar.

Until university, the French question didn't require a stance. But to be caught in French 100 by Calf-Roping majors could lead to serious physical reprisals. French students had to think fast on their feet. Black-stetsoned students roamed the hallways of the Fine Arts Building, their eyes narrowed to gunfighter slits:

"What course would you be takin', Slim?"

"Snake Handling and The Lord 103." (Only fools would answer, "French 100.")

An uneasy look faded into an imperceptible nod. "Me, I ain't big on reptiles."

Confrontations of this type were common, but offset by the rewards of cheap wine and pale women from French 239 *("Existentialisme")* who claimed to read Camus — in the original — and tended to prove that Tim Garneau was right. Pale women aside, there was still the awkward task of actually learning the language. As the Camus-toting women became less mysterious and the language failed to follow suit, there was an exodus from the course that left only those who could already speak French. The rest of us decided that perhaps chain-smoking Gitanes was really all that was needed to evoke the Gallic style.

After university, I settled into life in Calgary, a city that accords French the same official status as Latin. Life in Alberta has never been conducive to learning French. Even ordering food loses some of its cachet when it's *bateau o' boeuf* in a restaurant called Steers 'n' Beers. Still, I felt the heat was off and contented myself with learning the local dialect ("Punched a duster High River way, figger to mebbe frac the sucker or whipstock a wildcat into the next lease."), doomed to rope and ride without a hint of *je ne sais quoi.*

SOME ENGLISH SPOKEN HERE
by Mark Abley

In some parts of the West, people speak some kind of English. Scattered pockets of resistance exist throughout the prairies: Portage la Prairie, Dauphin, Qu'Appelle, Perdue, Leduc, and a few others. Visitors to those communities should speak French only. (To be sure, check to see whether the local Century 21 agent is selling real estate or *Riel état.*) Ask at a bar or bistro for *le plein,* and at a gas station for *un gros Mol* — not to be confused with big Molly, who hangs out at the bus depot.

Some western place names will baffle any tourist unfamiliar with French. In northern Alberta, Lac la Biche means "absent the bishop." Likewise, in Saskatchewan, Ile à la Crosse signifies "island at the crucifix." Across the next provincial boundary, The Pas doesn't mean "the pass," it means "the father" in honour of a missionary priest hurrying off to Lac la Biche.

Even in towns with English names like Esterhazy and Wetaskiwin, residents will be glad to practise their French with total strangers from Ontario and Quebec.

If you don't know French, try Ukrainian. This is extremely useful for the purposes of seduction. The exception: Esquimalt, B.C., where the *lingua franca* is Inuktituk.

EDMONTON vs. CALGARY
THE WHOLE TRUTH
by Ron Marken

Anyone east of Lloydminster or west of Canmore will not know Alberta's two most burning questions: How much is left in the Heritage Fund? and Which is the better city, Calgary or Edmonton? Rumor has it that the United Nations General Assembly intends to settle the second of these earthshaking issues in its next session. Until then, here are the facts.

Edmonton has been ticked off for fifty years because all the world knows the magic words "Calgary Stampede," but thinks Edmonton is a military outpost in Latvia. It was for this reason — rather than to honor the Royal visit of King George VI in 1938 as officials claimed — that Edmonton started a rivalry between the two cities. "I am the best!" bleated Edmonton into the ear of a bemused and indifferent monarch. Calgary was not informed.

Ten years later, Calgary learned of the debate and, to prove their superiority, knocked down six old buildings and knocked up ten office towers. Edmonton writhed with jealousy because its biggest building was the MacDonald Hotel. So, Edmonton leveled Jasper Avenue. No one was watching, though.

What irritated Edmonton the most was that it had the legislature, was the capital city, and was home to the provincial university. Still, no one beyond Wainwright had heard of it. Meanwhile, Calgary was famous as far as Fort Worth. Even Montrealers knew of its existence; they thought men wearing high heels and big white hats were chic.

Edmonton had no choice. It poked holes in every acre of land for fifty miles around (using Oklahoma and Texas money) and struck natural gas. Then it struck oil! Finally its time had come; it was the Oil Capital of Canada.

The mayor of Calgary lazily swung his cowboy boots off his desk and sent a telegram to J.R. Ewing. Ten minutes later, all the world's oil companies had built their head offices in Calgary (a city whose total oil production rivals that of Cambridge, England). Calgary called Edmonton and said, in a friendly voice with just a trace of an Oklahoma accent, "You might be the Oil Capital of Canada, sweetie, but down here, we *own* the oil."

Edmonton writhed again. So it bought fifty-five young Americans, called them "Eskimos," and used them to beat up on the rest of Canada all through the '50s. (There are no real Eskimos in Edmonton, of course, but the name suggested it was cold as hell in Edmonton and therefore Edmonton was really tough.) Although Calgary didn't really want to, it also bought fifty-five young Americans with some petty cash from Standard. They were called the "Stampeders" (naturally). They proceeded to lose all their games — with style. Everyone still loved Calgary.

Desperate by now, Edmonton went all the way. It tried to rival the Calgary Stampede with a forced extravaganza called "Klondike Days." The real Klondike, in the Yukon, thought it was pretty ridiculous, and Calgary ignored it completely. It was too busy putting on the one show that every man, woman, and child on earth wants to see: the Calgary Stampede.

One February day, Edmonton's phone rang. "Howdy, sweetie." It was Calgary. "How's the weather up there? We're havin' us a chinook and I'm in my swimmin' pool." In Edmonton, the mercury hovered around minus fifty, but Edmonton (unable to buy a chinook for love or oily money) now bragged about being *hardier* than that candy-assed Calgary. No one believed that. Edmonton got so angry it brought fifteen Quebecers, ten Saskatchewanians, and a gawky kid from Ontario.

"See, here!" shouted Edmonton into the phone. "I've got you at last! I have an NHL team and they are goin' ta kick the ass of everyone on this continent. No one can say, 'Where's Edmonton?' now. I'll show you!" Calgary, puzzled by this challenge, absentmindedly bought an entire NHL team from Atlanta, Georgia (famous for its hockey players), and continues a losing sports tradition.

But still, the world loves Calgary and hates Edmonton. It will never change. And even Edmonton's latest boast — "I have the longest street full of churches in all of Christendom and the biggest shopping mall in the entire galaxy!" — somehow fails to electrify. Calgary got more attention by going broke. Edmonton writhes again. See you at the Stampede.

ALBERTA'S PLACE IN HISTORY
BUILDING A REPUTATION
by Mark Abley

Albertans so love the past that they spend millions of dollars creating replicas of buildings they have just torn down. In Edmonton, an "old house" is one built before the reign of Peter the Great and his Heritage Fund. Today, people come from as far away as Nanaimo and Yellowknife to worship at the largest shrine in Canada: the West Edmonton Mall.

"The bathroom is on the right, son. The West Edmonton Mall is to the left."

Watch the expressions of rapture on the faces of the believers as they stream through the marble portals and wander the sacred shopping precincts. The fountains, modelled after those of Versailles, double as fonts into which new-born consumers are dipped, clutching their charge cards. Before making their sacramental purchases, most of the congregation pause to watch the young priests conduct a mysterious ceremony on skates. The high priest wears a surplice bearing the holy number 99 — a stern reminder of how many dollars each communicant must spend per hour.

WESTERN TRIVIA QUIZ

1. Is curling:
   a) The sport of kings?
   b) The sport of queens?
   c) The sport of kins and kinettes?

2. Who is Roy Romanow?
   a) A relative of the Tsar of Russia.
   b) The inventor of "baco'bits."
   c) A Ukrainian Robert Redford look-alike.

3. How big is the Expo 86 deficit — as of this moment?
   a) Bigger than a bread box.
   b) Smaller than Bill Bennett's ego.
   c) About twice the size of — say — Yugoslavia.

4. Who owns Alberta?
   a) Texas.
   b) Saudi Arabia.
   c) All of the above.

5. Why did they buy it?
   a) It was either that or buy Saskatchewan.
   b) They wanted Airdrie and Sundrie.
   c) Only Saudi Arabia could afford to mount the Calgary Olympics.

6. How much will the Calgary Olympics lose?
   a) Half the Heritage Fund.
   b) One-quarter of Pierre Trudeau's salary.
   c) Enough to have bought Banff back from the Brewsters.

7. Name all the western Canadian cities over 100,000 without an NHL franchise?
   a) Saskatoon.
   b) Regina.
   c) All of the above.
   d) Who gives a damn?

8. Who staged the Peter Pocklington kidnapping?
   a) His mother.
   b) Joe Schocter.
   c) Dave Semenko.

9. Why did they return him?
   a) They wanted to watch him run for the leadership of the PCs.
   b) God knows.
   c) Even God doesn't know.

10. What is "Boh"?
    a) A northern male.
    b) An extremely boring sex star.
    c) The front half of a hunk.
    d) An ex-great beer.

11. Where is Spuzzum?
    a) Only your doctor knows
       for sure.
    b) I don't know but I hope it
       isn't catching.
    c) Just beyond Hope.

12. Does Gimli have an airport?
    a) Yes, but only Air Canada
       can find it.
    b) No, and Air Canada still
       found it.
    c) Maybe, and let's hope it
       has a gas station.

13. Is there life after Victoria?
    a) Yes. It's called Hawaii.
    b) Yes. It's called Socred
       Patronage.
    c) No. There is not even life
       in Victoria.

14. How many real estate agents
    are there in Calgary?
    a) One for every 2.4 people.
    b) Not enough to sell
       PetroCan to Gulf.
    c) Not enough to prevent
       Marc Lalonde from selling
       them all down the Bow
       River.

15. How many Manitobans does
    it take to produce "Hymn
    Sing"?
    a) I am already bored by the
       question.
    b) More than will ever
       watch.
    c) 184 CBC employees to
       justify funding for the
       blandest program on air.

16. How many Prince Georgians
    does it take to chop down a
    tree?
    a) None. Prince George uses
       chain saws.
    b) None. The premier has
       closed Prince George.
    c) None. Prince George is on
       strike.

17. What word most commonly
    describes Saskatchewan,
    "Land of Outdoor Fun"?
    a) Flat.
    b) Boring.
    c) Ugly.
    d) Half-full of commie pinko
       creeping socialis hordis.

18. When does the last tourist
    leave Churchill, Manitoba?
    a) After the arrival of the
       first polar bear.
    b) Ahead of the first polar
       bear — running.
    c) Inside the first polar bear.

19. Why does Canada train the
    RCMP in Regina?
    a) There are millions of flat
       acres to practise their
       musical: "RIDE!"
    b) Regina is the outlaw
       capital of Canada.
    c) With so many socialists,
       someone must defend the
       Right.

20. Do you remember the Red
    River Valley?
    a) No, but can I just hum
       along?
    b) I can't even remember our
       anniversary!
    c) Would you mind repeating
       the question?

WESTERN CULTURE
by Michael Gillgannon

The Westerner's automatic response to culture is "Gesundheit!" The proper utterance should be, "Oh piffle! My subscription to the Symphony Society is deucedly close to dead. I'd better renew straightaway."

There *are* symphony societies in the West. Look in the Yellow Pages under "Polkas & Misc." Join them and learn how to pronounce words like *Mozart, concerto* and *viola.* And when gossiping about the conductor's relationship with the cellist, remember: in the Symphony Society the word is *piquant,* not *steamy.*

And there are symphony society pancake breakfasts. These open-air affairs cause Westerners to congregate in terrifying, huge packs. What do Westerners do at these pancake breakfasts, besides eat pancakes in vast quantities? First, gossip about the Symphony's conductor (see *piquant,* above). Second, compare incomes. The biggest income gets to tell a Ukrainian joke.

When they run out of pancakes, it's time for the ribbon-cutting ceremony at the Co-op's new Truck Battery Department. The Co-op president praises truck batteries in western society, the ribbon is cut, all breathing stops as the severed pieces flutter to the ground, and the travelling symphony strikes up a gut-stirring rendition of *Prelude to the Afternoon of a Fawn* or *Ninety-nine Bottles of Beer on the Wall.* Then everyone goes home to check the mail.

The more mail you get the more cultured you are. Especially if it's from American Express, Birks, or the Symphony Society. *De rigeur* is an invitation to view the works of a well-starved artist whose medium is beer bottle caps stuck together with cow patties.

Most Westerners own a cow. A cow guards the house, eats dandelions, manures the garden of culturally OK vegetables like okra and watermelon, and supplies milk in summer, ice cream in winter, and yogurt in spring and fall. The udder (that thing down there that looks like the glove the doctor wears when he wants to investigate what you don't want investigated) can also be used as a football with handles.

The symphony open-air pancake breakfast

Don't think that the subject at hand, culture (Gesundheit!), is exhausted, because curling is on almost the very tippy-top of the list.

Curling is a, shall we say, sport. But a cultured sport, like dominoes on ice. There's this rock or stone thing with a handle on it, and you slide it, and your teammates sweep a path for it as it meanders down the ice, and it hits or maybe doesn't hit some other rocks, so you win or lose or something, and you go next door to the pub.

Want more culture? The West *teems* with that Gesundheit word.

For instance: Lollygagging around the shopping mall; collecting western things like barbed wire and locust shells; sunbathing in the satellite dish; stocking the freezer with fresh-killed moose (In northern Alberta, never greet the locals with "Hello." Always say, "Got yer moose yet?"); going to the Lake (all lakes in the West are called "The Lake"); changing your motor oil and dumping the old oil in the alley; standing upright in the wind that never stops.

Visiting a
Manitoba
Art Gallery

And then there is British Columbia, that wet country Texans think of as being in South America. Eastern Canadians know it as a wacky place across the mountains and over the rainbow, somewhere west of Moose Jaw. We all know about its majestic majesty and vista-filled vistas, but what about its Gesundheit word? Is it possible for B.C. to have thundering waterfalls, mighty Douglas firs, pounding surf *and* culture? Yes, it is. Here is a complete list of culture in B.C.:

— the Vancouver Symphony Orchestra
— everything in Victoria
— muffin shops
— everything edible in the Okanagan Valley
— any person who knows how to spell (and pronounce) Tsawwassen
— all totem poles not manufactured in Taiwan
— standing in the rain at a bus stop and noticing moss growing on your north side and letting it grow because you know all living things have a right to life
— having a two-boat garage
— shopping underground in Vancouver and never coming up again
— having the opportunity to force a recreational vehicle off the road and down a mountainside, but not doing it
— having the opportunity to force a recreational vehicle off the road and down a mountainside, and doing it, and what's more, liking it

In any Royal Commission on Culture (Gesundheit!), the West will always sit tall in the saddle.

WESTERN CULTURAL EQUIVALENTS

Finding the best seats for the Eston Gopher Derby.

EAST	WEST
* Stratford Shakespeare Festival	** Kindersley Goose Festival
* The National Ballet	** The Craven Jamboree
* The National Film Board	** Winnipeg Folk Festival
*** Ontario Provincial Election	** Calgary Stampede
* Montreal Jazz Festival	* Carrot River Oldtime Fiddling Contest
**** Hamilton Acid Rain Dip	** Vancouver Polar Dip
* Quebec Winter Carnival Canoe Race	** Nanaimo to Duncan Bathtub Race
*** The Queen's Plate	*** Eston Gopher Derby
* *Surfacing* by Margaret Atwood	* Annual Re-surfacing of Dave Barrett

Legend:
 * funded lavishly by the Canada Council
 ** not funded at all by the Canada Council
 *** ought to be funded by the Canada Council
 **** ought to *pay* the Canada Council

SEX

by Mark Abley

Most Westerners like it. But try getting them to admit it. Out of natural discretion, a memory of Bible College, or a desire not to offend the neighbours, they speak in a variety of private terms derived mostly from Ukrainian.

Don't ask a pretty prairie girl if she'd like to come up and see your etchings. Look her in the eyes and say, "Would you like to sample my perogy?" If she likes you, she'll probably reply, "Sure — and you must taste my verenyky!" The two of you will soon make borscht together.

Through the endless months of winter, Westerners indulge in a multitude of orgies. These are known by the codeword "bonspiel" (literally, "good play . . ."). Admission to these events may be difficult for outsiders, but travellers to a town with a large "bonspiel" ought to remember these rules: 1. don't be afraid to break the ice; 2. be ready to join in a foursome; 3. carry a stiff broom. Prudence forbids me to say more.

The red-light districts of the West aren't as obvious as those in Toronto and Montreal. Nevertheless, they exist; look out for the nearest "holoptsi." In Winnipeg, heterosexual visitors should avoid the provincial legislature, where the golden statue of a naked boy makes the prevailing tendencies all too clear.

Foreplay Western style.

WESTERN CUISINE
by Mark Abley

Even more than bonspiels and Ukrainian immersion, prairie men and women enjoy their meat. Many a Westerner has followed the ancient custom of being buried with a steak in his heart. The guests at the funeral then eat a piece of "Saskatoon Bury Pie," the ingredients of which remain a secret.

A traditional way for Westerners to show their affection for eastern Canada is to go into a restaurant and order "a beef against Ontario." Visitors may like to reciprocate in kind. Just wait until the waitress arrives to take your order; then bang your fist on the table and say in a loud voice, "I've got a beef against Alberta!" If you want a plateful of pork, try announcing, "Alberta is a pig of a place!" (This doesn't work so well with lamb, but sheep are uncommon on the prairies anyway.)

The favourite drinks in the West are beer, milk, rye, and coffee. It may be unwise for tourists to mix all four at a single sitting. Teetotallers should pay a side-trip to Milk River in southern Alberta, which is dry even in the years when there hasn't been a drought. Ask for a croissant and a hot chocolate in the beverage room of the Milk River Hotel.

When in doubt, be brave. There is more to western cuisine than Colonel McDonald and Ronald Sanders. You might like to sample a Winnipeg specialty: Manitoba goldeyes with hot fudge sauce. But a word of warning: although a prairie chicken is indeed a kind of bird, a prairie oyster is *not* a shellfish.

And be careful who you approach for verenyky.

THE MANHANDLER
A RECIPE FOR PRAIRIE OYSTERS

What do fun bars in Toronto, New Brunswick swamps, and the coastal waters off Newfoundland have in common with the prairies? Food. Rare tasty treats for the strong at heart, the venturesome, and the starved. Easterners bored with the well-chewed tastes of sushi, fiddleheads, and cod cheeks will thrill to the as yet little-known prairie oyster.

PRAIRIE OYSTERS

You wants to catch a few young bulls, you see, because they got balls that's mighty testy, er tasty. When you clips them parts the little critters (the bulls that is) grow fat and turn into market steers. If they gets to hang onto their gonads the horny sons-a-bs spend all their time chasin' cows and gettin' skinny livin' the wild life. And there ain't no money in that!

Now makin' prairie oysters is easier said than wrote. But if ya follows these few easy steps, chances are there'll be nothin' to it.

First, and very important, a strong anaesthetic is necessary — ya gotta make things numb. Any cheap rye will do. Drink half a quart, straight. Now ya can imagine, most bulls ain't too fond of having their parts snipped off, but if ya catches one on a cold fall morning, hours before they've spied their first cow of the day, it makes the task much easier. Ya creeps along the grass comin' up behind the bull. Yer knife should be clenched in yer teeth. By now, ya should have a clear view of the items, they're usually just hangin' around, sleepin' it off. Ya comes up real slow and quiet, ya see, gettin' closer and closer. Now yer within strikin' distance. Should the big fella suddenly turn his head and spy you starin' hungrily up at his parts breezin' in the wind, play dead; curl up in a ball and freeze. If that don't work, offer him some of that rye. If he's still givin' ya a stiff eye, you'd best drink that rye and run. Barrin' any problems, such as I've just described, take your knife and with a real quick slice cut them little morsels off and head for the hills. Needless to say, ya could be runnin' a long time on the prairies.

Once ya got yer items, be sure to soak 'em in salt water. No one really understands why, but a cowboy friend o' mine says it might be dangerous to find out. Anyway, accordin' to the recipe, it's gotta be done.

Full view of prairie oysters.

Before ya actually whips those fresh morsels inta the fryin' pan, ya gotta remove any loose stuff like . . . like . . . well, there just ain't no delicate way of sayin' it — tubin' an' tissue. I always shut my eyes for that part. Then I take another swig of rye. Well now, yer gettin' closer to the time when you can really sink yer teeth inta the . . . er . . . meat. Make sure ya got that campfire sizzlin' hot before ya dip the little critter's manlies inta a mixture of egg and milk. Then roll 'em up in some cracker crumbs so's they're cleverly disguised as real food. Now when the butter's slidin' around the skillet like a frog on an icy pond, ya quickly throw the battered balls inta the fryin' pan. Be sure to stand upwind from the fire. When the outsides is nice and crisp and the insides are re—e—al tender, ya know ya got yerself a dandy cowboy snack.

So, the next time them eastern bastards talk about their fancy croissants, light wine and raw fish, you tell 'em it takes balls to eat prairie oysters . . . in more ways than one; I mean two, or, oh hell, ya know what I mean.

GO WEST DESPERATE WOMAN GO WEST

by Patrick Lane

You're thirty-three, free, and a woman of the New World. But let's face it, there just aren't any men in your town. It's time to head west where there are male bodies that don't carry briefcases, rugged faces whose tans haven't come from a sunlamp, and hairy knees that don't have that grinding gravel sound that comes from jogging beside the Rideau Canal.

On the Great Plains there are men who still believe that opposites attract. Men who like their loving traditional. It's true. You look into your mirror when you're peeling off your makeup and shaking the croissant crumbs from your blouse. You say: "I'm tired of having men friends whose failed love affairs are not with me."

Your girlfriend Kathy says it. She's drunk and she says it. *"THERE'S NO MEN HERE!"*

So you march into your boss's office and resign. No more having to listen to yourself try to speak French. It's *GO WEST* almost-middle-aged-woman. You've read the about the rugged ranchers of the South Saskatchewan in *Equinox*, you've bought designer cowboy boots, you've even thought of getting a bluebird tattooed on your left breast. You're ready!

When you board Pacific Western Airlines, you say: "No more spritzers and quiches. No more Fellini, Fassbinder, and Bergman reruns. To hell with Virginia Woolf, George Sand, Susan Sontag, and Margaret Atwood. I want to be an edible woman! I've put my bra back on!"

You're still the girl who burned her bra in front of the Parliament buildings; the girl who said for all the world to hear: "I'm free." You're still her. Down deep you're still Sgt. Pepper's One-Girl-Band.

You're in Regina! So there are no restaurants, movie theatres, book stores, galleries, clubs, trees, hills, rivers, birds or squirrels. So there aren't any houses older than you. You sit in your new apartment with its avocado plant and satin pillows. You've got a map that looks like a blow-up of a triscuit. You're planning your weekend.

It's summer. It's Agribition! There's a rodeo, a midway. There are farmers, ranchers, and cowboys!

You dress careful-ly in the designer jeans from which you've strip-ped the labels, and the little blouse checkered in red and white with the buttons undone down to the place where your bluebird would have been. You pull on your new pink cowboy boots. You climb under the cute cowboy hat. Forget the dust that clogs your pretty nostrils, the wind that dries your skin. Forget the sun that makes your head sweat and ruins your perm.

Hanging out at the pig barn.

You decide to hang out at the pig barn. Then you saunter along the stalls at the Hereford Show. You chew a blade of dessicated grass at the tractor-pull. Finally you sit at a dusty table and drink warm Pepsi with a plate of glutinous perogies, making sure your boots peek out invitingly.

You wait for someone to speak to you. You want to hear: *YOU'RE MY KIND OF GAL!* or *HEY THERE, LITTLE LADY!* or *HOW ABOUT A RIDE ON MY STALLION, PRETTY WOMAN!*

But it doesn't happen.

There are men, but they're looking at tractors and other strange machines. When you walk close to these men they mumble and look off into the distance, leaving you to stare at their herbicide-stained little buns, their broad shoulders, their red necks, their big hands that could smack a cow on the ass or scrunch a pig's ear.

And who are those tough-looking women who look like they could bend the bumper on a BMW with their little fingers? Are those their wives?

The closest you have come to conversation was with a skinny guy in jogging shorts at the ticket stand who asked you where you were from. When you told him, he overcharged you for a seat at the rodeo a mile away from the cowboys and the Brahma bulls. You've eaten your lipstick off. You're tired.

Creating the "new you" at Regina's leading Salon de Beaute.

The next day you go to a bar and meet a guy with a little blue cap in his back pocket that says Moose Jaw Jamboree. It's a farmer's cap and it's cute. You take the plunge. You invite him back to your apartment. You've made sure there's a bottle of rye and coke in the fridge. He's sitting on your new couch and he's talking and you're thinking: Please, let it be tonight!

But, instead of talking in that deep, sexy western voice you loved back in the bar, he's started to cry. Little sobs. He's telling you he wants to come out of the closet. All those years on the combine listening to the CBC have made him realize he's different and he wants your help because you're from Back East and you'll understand. He wants to talk about his mother!

It's been six months now. You're writing to Kathy. Do you tell her it's hell out West? No. You tell her you're having the time of your life. You tell her it's wildcat drillers, cowboys, and wild, wild men. Sure, it's just a little lie but you don't want Kathy to say, "I told you so." And you haven't tried everything. There's still a lot of West out there. You've heard of Vancouver. You've seen the pictures of Stanley Park. There are men there too. And maybe they're not what you think they are. Maybe. Just maybe.

In B.C., men are attracted to old-fashioned "girls" who own vintage sports cars and large yachts.

THE MACHO MEN OF THE WEST

As you journey west, you will be delighted to discover that nearly half the people you meet will be men. Western men are famous in song, story, and cliché. "Go West, young man," urged the first publishers of *Encyclopedia Britannica,* "Go West." The West has been filling with young men every since — but it's far from full.

The West needs thousands of wives, helpmates and homemakers. It even elects a couple of women to the legislature periodically. Western men, in their desperation, have been known to order women out of catalogues, tear women from the centres of magazines, and worship women on record jackets.

In the stirring masculinity of its men, the West truly puts its best face forward. These are manly men, mighty men, muscular men. All right, admit it — they are Macho Men, men who intimately know the hidden ways of air, earth, beasts, trees, and fish. Their strong round arms shine in the sun like marble. Their piercing blue eyes penetrate the secretest depths of the soul of the universe. They clasp their friends to their bosoms with hoops of steel. One of them is a Liberal.

Macho Alberta cowboy.

Macho B.C. lumberjack.

Macho Saskatchewan
snow plow driver.

Macho Winnipeg
Goldeye fisherman.

Macho prairie farmer.

Macho Hornby Island, B.C. artist.

DEAR BRONWYN
HOW AN EASTERNER COPED IN THE WEST
by Hildy Rhodes

May 1985

Dear Bronwyn,

A year ago we were tiddly over our sherry at the Granite Club, and now, thanks to my Hugh's impetuosity, I'm the *compleat* prairie housewife. Remember how dear Miss Moodie at school used to tell us over and over again: "Many things look well at a distance that are quite nasty when near?" Of course she was warning us against venturing out of Rosedale and dating boys whose names ended with "chuk" or "onini," but, oh Bronnie, how right she was! "Saskatchewan" has a nice iambic ring in a geography book, but no one here has even *heard* of Bishop Strachan School.

Life here is so . . . so *alternate*, I don't know where to begin.

Remember Fred's lovely Cobb salad at the Granite Club? Remember how, when we were feeling very naughty, we'd have a glass of Chablis to wash it down? Well, meat and potatoes, and plenty of them, that's how these solid sons of the soil stoke their engines. And in rural Saskatchewan, there is no such thing as "a glass of wine." An aperitif is totally unheard of. However, a bottle of #1 Hard (an amazingly *soothing* rye whisky) is considered just the ticket to wash down anything from fried eggs and bacon at dinner (served at noon!) to a midnight lunch of roast chicken (real range chicken), perogies (quaint Ukrainian crêpes), and cabbage rolls (no civilized equivalent). So, as Miss M. always told us, "One does one's best."

Speaking of doing one's best — last Saturday night, your former Head Girl won a belly-bumping contest at the Blucher Dine and Dance. Oh, Bronnie, I can *see* you *scrinching* your nose at this — the way you used to when you'd have to say, "Blessed are the poor," in dear Miss M.'s Religious Knowledge class. So perhaps I'd better take you to the Dine and Dance slowly.

First, *everybody* in Saskatchewan curls *constantly* from October to March. You can tell the softball season has ended and curling has begun when the ladies stop coming to dances in their baseball jackets and change to their stretch 'n' sew pant suits, their ankle socks, their pumps, and their curling sweaters. And all the mummies here wear those cunning buttons with pictures of their hockey-playing offspring. Bronnie, the buttons are sweet. Really!

Hughie and I were a hit from the moment we pulled into the parking lot for the Dine and Dance. (People here do not "drive cars." They "own vehicles," and the vehicle of choice in Blucher is the half-ton, a sort of elegant pickup truck.) Well, Hughie and I have a new half-ton, so all our stout rural friends were quickly in the parking lot "looking her over," as they say here. "Her" is the pronoun of choice on the prairies: "I filled her; I flooded her; I tuned her up." After the men had pronounced "her" sound, and the ladies had pronounced "her" cute, they offered us some of those "darling fuzzy dice to hang from the mirror to keep it from looking so bare."

Anyway, after our new vehicle had been found acceptable, we embarked on the dance part of the Dine and Dance. Bronnie, I won't fib you. Your ex-Head Girl, Hildy Rhodes, got absolutely squiffed at the Blucher Dine and Dance. Cherry brandy is really quite a nice drink, and Saskatchewan rurals are most hospitable.

So, graciously, I mixed and I toasted and I danced to a quite wonderful local group called the Moms and Pops (more accurately, *the* Mom and Pop — he on saxophone, with a moustache like Tom Selleck's; she on piano with a moustache better than Tom Selleck's). Just before lunch, Aubrey Hunt, our neighbour to the north (an absolute mountain of a man) proposed a special treat for "a nice little girl from Toronto (loud guffaws) who came to her senses and moved to Saskatchewan (loud applause)." Bronnie, I didn't mind that. It was, after all, said in fun, and as Miss M. always said, "Humour is the leaven that allows our souls to rise." I didn't even mind that the contest was somewhat brutish. Aubrey would take on any challenger; they would run at each other from the opposite sides of the room and collide — belly first — until one of the contestants was flattened.

So dear Hugh, who was a little squiffed himself, took up the challenge, and Aubrey *turned him down* because, and I quote, "Hugh, you're a nice fella but they didn't teach you about belly-butting at that fairy boys' school you went to in Toronto!" Bron, every boy I ever knew went to Upper Canada College (well, maybe a few went to Ridley), but I felt the honour of our way of life had been impugned. So I challenged our neighbour!

I challenged a 250-pound Saskatchewan farmer to a belly-butting contest! The Mom and the Pop stopped playing. The glasses of #1 Hard and cherry brandy paused in mid-air. I was afraid. But then I heard Miss Moodie's dear voice in that hushed curling-rink-dance-hall, that dear voice saying, "A Bishop Strachan girl is never without resources." Bronnie, do you remember that awful girl from Havergal whose father owned some gold mines up north — the one who was such an incredibly unethical field hockey player? Do you remember Miss M. telling us that when good sportsmanship fails, there's a tiny little trick one can do with one's knee, a kind of quick vertical move to the front of the bloomers that will chasten a girl who does not play by the rules. Well, Bronnie, I gave Aubrey the quickest vertical move in Saskatchewan to the front of the bloomers. I chastened him to the floor.

Well, Bron, I must scoot. Aubrey is coming over to rototill my garden. He has been a perfect lamb since the Dine and Dance. He promised to help Hugh with seeding if I teach *his* five girls field hockey and the rules of life according to Miss M. She taught us well.

Hugs to all.

Yours ever,

Hildy

NEWSWORTHY ORGANS
THE WESTERN MEDIA
By Grindley Matthews

"The media" is never used in western conversation except to scorn eastern propaganda: "I see where 'the media' says us farmers are getting too rich." Proper western usage is: "I hear on the radio that . . ." Careful attention to this practice, particularly where beer is served and no one wears a tie, will save the eastern visitor many painful experiences.

The careful Easterner will first consult the provincial highway map's list of nearby CBC stations. He can then be soothed by the programming deemed important by east-central Toronto, avoiding the laughable parochialism of western radio.

But turn the CBC *OFF* before entering a service station! Known CBC listeners suffer unspeakable consequences in vacant fields behind remote Gulf stations on the prairies.

ATTITUDES OF WESTERN MEDIA:

British Columbia: Trendy, flighty. Events east of the Rockies are reported in the same breath that announces railway accidents in India. Prone to hot-tub features. Thinks Nancy Green Raine is a great TV personality.

Alberta: Psychopathically hostile to all federal governments. Thinks everyone is interested only in their money. *Loved* Earnest C. Manning. Every fifty years advocates change in provincial government.

Probably.

Saskatchewan: Fashionably left. Journalists wearing blue jeans discuss current events in grimy pubs. Saskatchewan's media style characterized by native daughters and sons Zena Cherry, Dr. Foth, and Eric Malling.

Manitoba: Knows it's been left out of what's really happening. Fiercely proud of ethnic restaurants. Has never recovered from losing David Steinberg. Most famous Manitoba TV program: "Hymn Sing."

WHERE TO READ IN WESTERN CANADA

Vancouver Sun: The rich, fat paper of B.C. The only *Sun* without a curvaceous citizen on page three (there are 10,000 curvaceous citizens on the street outside). Good used waterbed ads and great deals on rusted-out Hondas.

Calgary Herald: Also rich and fat. Started a colourful tradition with the 1922 reporter, Chief Buffalo Child Long Lance, who threw a bowling ball with a burning 'fuse' of oil-soaked rags into a city council meeting.

Edmonton Journal: Grey, dull, resentful of the *Herald*. Still fears the *Edmonton Bulletin*. Announced it would be Lougheed's unofficial opposition. No one noticed. Now concentrates on stories about ladies of ill-repute.

Regina *Leader-Post*: "Voice of Saskatchewan." For years the legislature did not keep written records of debates, pasting and filing *Leader-Post* clippings instead. Main source of Saskatchewan news for the rest of Canada (i.e., has an out-of-province circulation of 7).

Saskatoon *Star-Phoenix*: From 1902 to 1906, misspelled its own name: "Phenix." Generally spells "consensus" as "concensus." Thinks "decimate" means "annihilate." Often prints same story twice. 97 percent news about NHL franchises and arenas; 2.9 percent news about Colin Thatcher; .08 percent provincial news; .01 percent national and international news.

The Western Producer: Published in Saskatoon, weekly, with the latest freight rates and year-old Garfield cartoons. Outwardly respectable, yet gives disconcerting glimpses of raw passions raging in isolated farmhouses: "WANTED. Healthy hard-working companion for 1200-acre mixed farm. Non-smoker, non-drinker. Tractor an asset. Please send photo of tractor."

Winnipeg Free Press: Once the thundering voice of the West, with powerful editors. Now billed as western Canada's "national newspaper" — a bleat to which no one listens. After purchase by Thomson of Fleet, its horizons extend from the Grain Exchange to the Bay.

THE CLASSIFIEDS

ACREAGES FOR SALE

The City of Calgary. Valuable grazing land. 4589 acres. No trees. Several buildings. No reasonable offer refused. Asking $100.00/acre. Box 222, c/o *The Calgary Herald*.

PERSONAL OWNER & General Manager of phantom NHL hockey team seeks willing city of dupes. Write Box 1986, *Star-Phoenix*.

FREE TOURS

When visiting the West Edmonton Mall be sure to take time to tour the historic *outside* City of Edmonton. Lots to see, including the buildings and homes where people used to work and live before moving indoors to a climatically and culturally controlled environment. Bring a coat.

CIVIC DECLARATION

The mayor of the City of Vancouver declares the week of September 9 "Bubble Week." There will be open-air bubble baths, free bubble gum, massive bubble-blowing contests, and gallons of "bubbly" to be consumed. Said the mayor, in costume closely resembling the Michelin Man, "It's never been done before and we feel it will enhance our image as a bunch of 'airheads.'"

LOST

Believed lost in the vicinity of the Expo '86 site. The B.C. provincial budget for the next twenty years. Anyone possessing information on the whereabouts of these funds should notify the authorities.

LOST

Believed lost in the vicinity of the Kananaskis and various Olympic sites throughout Calgary. The Alberta provincial budget for the next thirty years. Information leading to the whereabouts of these funds should be directed to the proper authorities. A large reward is offered.

LOST

All hope for the Saskatchewan Roughriders.

NOTICE TO TENDERS

The City of Winnipeg invites tenders for the modernization of downtown comfort stations. Pits must conform to Department of Health depth standards of not less than five feet. Tenders must be delivered to the city clerk's office by midnight, May 15.

ESCORT SERVICE

Don't be lonely when visiting Victoria. Call Mildred at the Sunset Village Retirement Home. Bingo and shuffleboard with a flare most nights.

MISCELLANEOUS FOR SALE

Government going out of business. All government-owned campgrounds in Banff and Jasper available at attractive low cost. Buyer guaranteed annual revenue exceeding one million dollars. Contact Parks Canada for further details. Any offer accepted.

FOR SALE

All financial institutions headquartered in western Canada. Small down payment on approved credit. No questions asked. Certified cheques only, please.

FOR SALE

Due to cutbacks in the CBC budget, the corporation is forced to divest itself of some interests. For sale will be the facilities, transmitters, and staff in the three prairie provinces and in northern B.C. Due to the fact that the weather along the B.C. coast is eminently conducive to the health of our Toronto managerial staff in mid-winter, the facilities in Vancouver and Victoria will remain in operation. All regional programming will emanate from Toronto. Inquiries should be directed to the CBC.

WANTED

Professional hockey and football teams for Calgary.

ARE YOU THERE: Western mystic speaks with pilots of UFOs seen regularly hovering over Manitoba. Do you want to converse with these strange beings too? Write to me for interview. Box 666, Brandon, Manitoba. We are not alone!

SPORTS IN THE WEST
LOG DANCING AND WAGON WHEEL BINGO
by Willy Thomas

The indigenous people of western Canada heralded our strong sporting tradition. Indians played lacrosse — a creative use for old butterfly nets — and further north, Eskimos were involved in the ancient sport of high kicking a dried seal pancreas hanging from a stick.

One cold January evening, the wagon train carrying the early pioneers stopped in what is now Eyebrow, Saskatchewan. A group of boys strapped old barrel hoops to their boots, stuffed Eaton's catalogues down their pants, bought a dozen sticks at Northwest Canadian Tire, gathered up some frozen oxen chips, went down to the nearest pond (about a fifteen-mile walk) and invented real hockey.

Meanwhile, curling was in its rudimentary form. Pioneer women with cleaning complexes as big as the whole prairie sky began sweeping up the curling pond after the badly liquored men were done with their game. It wasn't long before they began sweeping up while the challenge was still in progress. The game had taken a giant sweep forward. It is that same kind of pioneer spirit and imagination that led bored sadists to televise the game.

As this band of sport enthusiasts migrated further west, curling and hockey took on new dimensions. Arenas were built on the sides of mountains, and it was in British Columbia where the idea to change ends in hockey was first introduced to even out the time spent skating uphill. This also led to the innovative, but unethical practice of using brooms with loose straws designed to stop the head-long rush of rocks down the ice. B.C. also claims to have coined the term "skip" to describe the evasive leaping action of those early curlers.

When our forefathers reached the coast they paused briefly to drink in the majesty of the great forests before they began hacking them down for Expo 86. Such was the birth of the forest industry and the many sports that developed from it. These include tap dancing on buoyant logs until your opponent falls in the water; climbing denuded trees with spiked boots and a rope belt to ring a bell, then leaping down. This places enough stress on the groin to make even today's viewer wince. There are incredible documented accounts of this event before they thought of stripping the branches from the trees. Then there is the challenge of chopping a log in half while standing on it. These one-footed lumberjacks went on to invent the popular B.C. water sport — slalom skiing.

Meanwhile, women were not idle. When not sweeping up the debris on curling rinks or bandaging their husbands' mutilated feet, they were busy inventing a blood sport of their own — bingo. It was a delighted family that greeted mother returning from bingo with a new butter churn, a patchwork quilt, or a wagon wheel won that night. Today, thanks to those early pioneers, bingo is big business (undoubtedly Mafia controlled), and draws more tour buses than Elvis Presley's Graceland.

In recent years, football has been added to the list of popular sporting attractions, to spite our British ancestors who tried to introduce lawn bowling and cricket unsuccessfully. In the West, football is a hard-hitting game. The East, ever-cunning, resorts to finesse. Small wonder that the roster of Canadians on an Eastern team consists of stockbrokers' sons who think pigskin has something to do with the commodities market. The hulking lads out of the West are sons of pig farmers, truck drivers, and ministers — men who have to be tough.

Not all western sports are *played* by Westerners. Those that aren't playing are watching. Western watchers take their sport straight, like rye from a quart thermos. Sport defines the watcher's rabid western regionalism. His enthusiasm starts in the pit of his stomach and spreads to his fists, tongue, knees, and groin. He cannot hear, and will not tolerate argument. In fact, today the ultimate western sport takes place when some poor wretch shouts "Go Argos" in Edmonton's Commonwealth Stadium. Bits of hair and clothing can still be seen floating in the air over Edmonton weeks later.

So we salute the free spirit of our pioneers, the oxen that supplied pucks, the glaciers that provided rubble for the first curling rocks, the electricity of a wagon train bingo parlor, and the men and women who got tougher as the going got tough.

When you're in Chilliwack, Nelson, Port Alberni, or Squamish, never ask a local citizen, "Do you come from B.C.?" No one *comes from* B.C. Everyone *goes to* B.C. The entire continent has an irresistible slope to the west and thousands of Canadians annually roll from right to left across the map, heading for the green and pleasant perfection that is British Columbia.

These migrations really annoy the 286 people who were actually *born* in B.C. If all the Maritimers, Quebecois, Ontariariarioans, and Flatlanders stayed home, there would be plenty of jobs for native British Columbians. As it is, "employment-enhancement-on-an-ongoing-basis" projects like razing forests and digging holes in mountains, have become costly ways of sustaining a primal economy.

So, those ingenious natives devised the ultimate job, the ultimate make-work scheme. They call it "Strike." It's B.C.'s revenge on the rest of the country.

DRIVING TO VICTORIA
ROCKY MOUNTAIN HIGH WAYS
by Ron Marken

To truly enjoy the west coast you must *earn* the right to bask on B.C.'s bikini-baking beaches. You have to get there the hard way — by car.

Prepare here for the shocks of alpine motoring in western Canada. So far your journey has been straightforward. You are travelling west. What could be simpler? Well, after you pass Canmore, Alberta, your trip will never be the same again.

Most drivers favour the white-knuckle grip. They are wise. Anyone who says, "There is nothing to fear," has never seen the town of Frank, Alta. One day, half a mountain fell down on Frank, burying the town, the road, and the train tracks. You must drive through six hundred miles of mountains. They can all fall down on you. Hundreds of signs warn, "Watch for Falling Rocks." These signs are not useful; they are gallows humour. When a falling rock has your number on it, watching won't stop it. When you pass such signs, murmur, "Yea though I walk through the valley of the shadow of death . . . " twice.

"Keep Right Except to Pass," say other signs. Not good advice. *Never* pass because someone will come around that curve and smash into you head-on. Passing is dangerous. It is also pointless. If you pass those four camper trailers, you will only overtake four more camper trailers a mile up the road. Mountains render camper trailers incapable of driving faster than 37 mph.

Fill up with gas at every second service station. The sun rises over the mountains at 11:30 a.m. and sets behind the other mountains at 12:09 p.m. every day, so locals never know what time it is. They start closing after sunset. You could be gasless and stranded anywhere between Vernon and Lulu.

Eighty percent of your trip will be on the *outer edge* of the road. When this happens, do *not* think, "I am moving at 40 mph, in a 3000 lb car, 18 inches from a sheer drop of 1500 feet. If a tire blew or a tie-rod snapped, I'd be as helpless as that rusted, burned-out wreck down there in the pine trees." That way madness lies. Unfortunately, you will be unable to think of anything else. So pretend you are in Winnipeg. Nobody ever fell out of Winnipeg.

Mountain blizzards are common, so carry tire-chains. You will not use them, but they could make you feel better. One man I knew drove five miles with tire chains. One came loose. He watched it tear his left front fender to shreds. From the inside. Maybe it's better to be stuck.

Just before you get to Vancouver, you will pass through Hell's Gate. It is your final test. If you survive Hell's Gate, you earn Paradise. By now,

Hell's Gate. Your final test.

you can't straighten your fingers. Your forearms tingle. Your eyes are gritty. Your neck muscles are solid knots. Your nerves whimper audibly. So much scenery has made your children hysterical. Your wife stopped talking six hours ago, right after the incident with the logging-truck. The transmission is making that funny "grrrrr" sound. The air conditioner quit yesterday. The car's interior resembles a microwave oven at full blast. The last gas fill-up cost you eighty cents a litre. There are no radio stations and you have had no news from the outside world since Cochrane.

Hell's Gate. First, a series of tunnels — dark, old, narrow, long tunnels. Then the boiling brown water of the Fraser River, angrier and angrier on your right. The canyon narrows. "Hell's Gate," "HELL'S GATE," **"HELL'S GATE!"** scream the signs. Left, right, left, left, right, you wheel. The cliffs now actually hang over you. You remember Frank.

Suddenly, it's over. Billions of mountains are behind you. You are on a green alluvial plain. You can drive just the way you drive in Halifax. You can smell the sea. Vancouver throbs its siren song of decadent pleasure just around the corner.

Unfortunately, you have no nerves left. Your idea of beauty is a pale white room, Muzak, and thin gruel. Vancouver will be wasted on you. You can now understand why there are so many old people in Victoria. They didn't intend to be old people in Victoria. Hale and hearty, they once set out to drive through the mountains; they are too terrified to drive back. So, when addressed, they can only murmur, "Victoria? Of course, it's absolute *heaven.*"

A survivor of the arduous mountain journey relaxes in Victoria

INTERVIEW WITH JOE BLOW
THE MAN WHO BLEW UP B.C. PLACE

A very special moment in Vancouver.

PAT MARSDEN: Joe Blow, how do you feel as the man who blew up the B.C. Place dome?

JOE: Well, Pat, it's, like, you know, a very special moment of memory in my life.

PAT MARSDEN: How did you feel, Joe, when you saw that old roof begin to rise?

JOE: It's hard to put into words, Pat, but probably marrying my beautiful wife Gladys comes closest.

PAT MARSDEN: Then how did you feel when management put you on waivers?

JOE: You know, Pat, like, it really didn't bother me all too much. 'Cause, you see, I've got other offers probably. When, like, you blow up something as important as a football stadium, agents come from all over the world, sort of.

JOHNNY ESAW: How do you feel about leaving B.C., Joe?

JOE: Me and Gladys have always had a yen for travelling, and, you know, there are rumblings that maybe, just possibly, Toronto might be in the market for a domed stadium. Mind you, they're pretty slow on things like that. I'm hoping Drapeau will move to Toronto and become mayor, so the dome plan can move ahead with all haste and waste. Then me and Gladys could retire in comfort.

A LETTER FROM BRITISH COLUMBIA

by Gail Bowen

Dear Margaret Rose:

How surprised you must be to hear from me! I know I promised dear Father Bill and the ladies at St. Luke's that I'd keep a trip diary, but there are some things that one cannot put in a diary that the Anglican women of Port Hope, Ontario, might read. And I've always felt that because you love dear Barbara Cartland's stories as I do, we two perhaps inhabit a larger world than the others. And, Margaret Rose, from the moment I crossed the border into British Columbia, I have been inhabiting a larger world.

First, I am travelling with a man — a very respectable one, of course — a widower. I was having breakfast in the dining car and I had my *Reader's Digest Illustrated Guide to Canada* open at page 180 for Kamloops, and Linton — that's my gentleman's name — sat down and we began to chat. There was nothing forward about it. You know how trains are and, of course, they are freer here in British Columbia. At any rate, Linton looked at my little book and asked me straight out if I wanted to see the real B.C. Well, at 70, adventures don't come every day, and I believe in taking the adventure God sends me. So I shut my guide, and I've been venturing ever since.

British Columbia is not at all that lotus land of blue skies and snow-capped mountains the IODE slide show would have us believe it is, but Linton says that once you get a sniff of the mountains and the summer fruit, you're seduced forever.

I can tell you first hand that Vancouver is not what our late King George and his sweet Elizabeth believed it to be — not at all. Remember that delightful film we showed of the 1939 Royal Tour at the Monarchist League? You will recollect that George VI saw Vancouver and said "I have never seen anything like it." Oh, the Royals always have such a way with words. And the Queen (always the *real* Queen to me and, I vouchsafe, to most of Port Hope) said in her spunky way, "This seems to me the place to live." Well, after seeing the real Vancouver, I can only echo the late King.

Oh, Margaret Rose, the people of Vancouver are so "laid back," to use their odious term, they are almost comatose. They live for the beaches and White Spot hamburgers and trips to Bellingham, Washington, to see spicy films.

"I do feel sorry for little Fernie, B.C."

I well remember that cold night that you and I, in mufti, picketed the Royal Theatre on Walton Street to protest the showing of that film where the young girl joked about losing her virginity. Well, Linton tells me that the young people of Vancouver think *virgin* is a term one applies to the wool in expensive ski-sweaters. Now although we believe a woman's loss of her jewel should not be taken lightly, here in British Columbia they take virginity casually. Probably someone is taking virginity casually even as I write.

I am told that Vancouver endures an average downtown rainfall of 58 inches every year. All I can say is *good!* If rain keeps young people from cavorting on the beaches half — no, seven-eighths nude, or from driving down to Bellingham to see films about sultans and harems, I do say, "Good for that rain!" I have seen those fine young boys with their gleaming bodies, brown and sleek in the sun that pulses down hot and penetrating on Kitsilano Beach. And if you could see those bronzed boys throbbing with life and tumescent with hope for a better world, you too would say, "Good for those 58 inches — those 58 inches that keep them indoors and safe." One cannot blame them. They are young, and what, after all, would they do indoors? Read the Vancouver papers? Hardly! Governments in Ontario or even Quebec could fall, and not a word of the event would appear in the Vancouver papers. I have read those papers and I know. I have seen those front pages that talk only of beach weather and water temperatures, and I have read, with sorrow, the personal columns. (So many entries are from young men who wish to meet others who "like leather.")

And if the newspapers are bad, the radio is worse. All those talkshows, "hotlines" they call them here, and everyone in such a fuss about the government all the time. As you know, I am not political. The *Book of Common Prayer* tells us to revere and uphold our government, and we all know of what government they are speaking. (If more people were reading their *Book of Common Prayer,* we wouldn't have a Liberal government in Ontario today.)

At any rate, dear, we can thank the good Lord that for forty-two years our good Tory premiers gave us a province where we could know and love all the people worth knowing and loving. That does not seem to be the case in British Columbia. I do not wish to speak ill of their premier, but his father's name was Wacky, and, as we well know, that sort of thing does run in families. And I do feel sorry for little Fernie, B.C. Apparently, in a fit of pique, Wacky's son, the current premier, left Fernie off the map altogether, and he wouldn't put them back on again until they threatened to secede.

Well, dear, tomorrow Linton and I are off to Victoria. You will recollect Rudyard Kipling's luscious description of Victoria: "To realize Victoria you must take all the eye admires in Bournemouth, Torquay, the Isle of Wight, the Happy Valley at Hong Kong, the Doon, Sorrento, Camp's Bay, add reminiscences of the Thousand Islands and arrange the whole around the bay of Naples with some Himalayas for the background."

Linton says that Kipling forgot to throw in the fact that on any given Sunday, fully 99 percent of the people taking high tea in the Empress Hotel couldn't find their bums with both hands in the full light of day. And Linton is from B.C., and he ought to know. Well, much love to you, Father Bill, and the girls at St. Luke's.

Ever yours,
Victoria.

WHY WESTERNERS LOVE HAWAII

Don't come West in the winter. It's closed. Everyone's in Hawaii. Everyone, that is, except the draft dodgers still living on Vancouver Island.

Why would anyone live in western Canada during the winter? On the prairies it's -55° from September to April, with an incessant wind known to squeeze pigs into pop bottles. In British Columbia it rains non-stop for seven months (the rest of the year it drizzles). And besides, the lovely state of Hawaii has hundreds of curling rinks and golf courses.

That's why people in Manitoba, Saskatchewan, and Alberta live in tents. Come mid-September everyone pulls out the pegs, folds up the Coleman stove, and catches a flight to Hawaii. At the same time, folks in British Columbia screw in the oar locks, drop in the oars, and row their houseboats to the islands of paradise.

Once in Hawaii, the days are happily spent cashing subsidy cheques for crops that didn't grow, selling handmade jewellery manufactured on some little hippie haven in the Georgia Strait, and sipping Canadian Club and Coke for less than it costs in Canada. There's no snow, no rain, no CBC-TV, no grasshoppers, and no news of Bill Bennett. All the Hawaiian papers carry the NHL statistics, and Hank Snow can be heard just about everywhere on the radio. White belts are still the rage in Hawaii, and God knows Westerners have lots of 'em, while polyester pant suits with multi-coloured floral patterns and bell bottoms ain't never goin' out of style. Hell, western Canadians don't even have to change their clothes. No wonder it's damn easy for Westerners to spend the winter in Hawaii.

Make sure to visit the West during the summer, but if you do decide to come in the winter, keep in mind that the power ain't hooked up and the water's been turned off.

PASS FOR A NATIVE
LEARN THESE TERMS

Bacon bits: A vile baked potato garnish invented by Roy Romanow to annoy admirers of Quebec *haute cuisine.* Contains no bacon.

Banker: Represents large, eastern organization. Job description: To "sell the farm" (see below).

Bannock: What pizza was before the Greeks came West.

Blizzard: In B.C., a thick shake or a carnival ride. In the rest of western Canada, a climatic condition that descends for a six-month period each year.

Brahma Bulls: A breed of bull noted for the particular flavor and texture of its parts, when used in Prairie Oysters. In cowboy lingo, a creature not to be messed with.

Doukhobor: An obscure Russian sect whose membership inexplicably take their clothes off and burn down buildings. Half of them vote Socred.

Fassbinder: Farm implement for accelerated distribution of organic fertilizer.

Field: Lovingly preserved park area. Used annually for "harvest" (see below).

Fodor: Writer of travel books. Married to "Modor," who writes cheap restaurant guides for hitchhikers.

Frank: The CPR's idea of an imaginative name for a B.C. mountain village.

Furrow: Straight line left in ground behind a plow. Throw seed into it. Throw fertilizer into it. Throw pesticide into it. Throw herbicide into it. Throw loose change into it. Wait three months. Yield: Millions of grasshoppers. Then "sell the farm" (see below).

Gallows Humour: Jokes about farming or the retention of capital punishment. Never funny.

Gopher: Neglected western cashcrop. The most plentiful species of livestock. Burrows help control the horse population.

Grasshopper Hatch: Microscopic plexiglass aperture in thorax of female grasshopper. With a magnifying glass, farmers are able to count unlaid eggs through it.

Harvest: Annual ritual in which billions of dollars worth of machinery collects millions of dollars worth of wheat.

Lotus Land: Corny name for Vancouver and Victoria, where natives use the term to explain why they can't answer their mail or defeat the Socreds.

Mountain: Rocks used to fill the B.C. interior. Certain to give the Laurentian-lover a fatal inferiority complex.

Oil Patch: The back of a Socred's easy chair.

PetroCan: A receptacle stored under any Calgarian's bed for midnight emergencies.

Portage and Main: Mean temperature, -47F; average wind speed, 87 kph. Canada's Bermuda Triangle.

Salmon Arm: A swim stroke developed by the Philosophy Department of Simon Fraser University. Widely copied in East Germany.

Snoose: Confection made from the droppings of young female goose. Delicious chewed.

"Sell the farm": Increasingly familiar euphemism for "hit rock bottom." Opposite of "Lotus Land" (see "Banker" above).

Stagette: All-girl party attended only by cheerleaders. Strong drink and monosyllabic jocks are not shunned.

Storm-stayed: Western equivalent of "I'm working late at the office tonight, dear."

Tie-rod: A small, usually metal rod used to tie bow-ties for a Western Senator who has never seen a tuxedo before.

Un Gros Mol: In western Canada, a large brown patch of hair on the skin; in Quebec a measure of a certain brand of beer.

THE WEST/EAST IMMIGRATION GAME

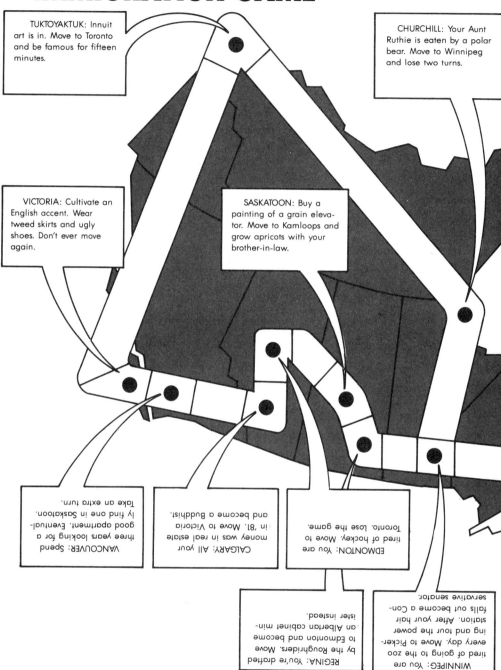

TUKTOYAKTUK: Innuit art is in. Move to Toronto and be famous for fifteen minutes.

CHURCHILL: Your Aunt Ruthie is eaten by a polar bear. Move to Winnipeg and lose two turns.

VICTORIA: Cultivate an English accent. Wear tweed skirts and ugly shoes. Don't ever move again.

SASKATOON: Buy a painting of a grain elevator. Move to Kamloops and grow apricots with your brother-in-law.

VANCOUVER: Spend three years looking for a good apartment. Eventually find one in Saskatoon. Take an extra turn.

CALGARY: All your money was in real estate in '81. Move to Victoria and become a Buddhist.

EDMONTON: You are tired of hockey. Move to Toronto. Lose the game.

REGINA: You're drafted by the Roughriders. Move to Edmonton and become an Albertan cabinet minister instead.

WINNIPEG: You are tired of going to the zoo every day. Move to Pickering and tour the power station. After your hair falls out become a Conservative senator.

WESTERN RULES:

1. The East has loaded the dice.
2. Roll the dice.
3. Defend the Crow!

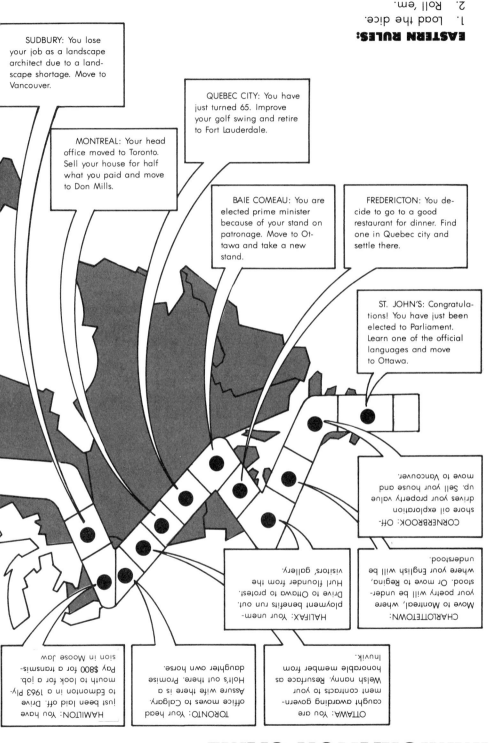

the WESTERNERS'
guide to
EASTERN
Canada

992

the
WESTERNERS'
guide to
EASTERN
Canada

edited by
Don Gillmor

Eden Press

Humor: That quality which appeals to a sense of the ludicrous; something that is or is designed to be comical or amusing.

THE WESTERNERS' GUIDE TO EASTERN CANADA
Edited by Don Gillmor

ISBN: 0-920792-53-7
© 1985 Eden Press, Inc.

Original cover cartoon: Tony Jenkins
Cover design and interior illustrations: Luba Zagurak
Book design: Luba Zagurak with Lynette Stokes
Photo credits: On pages 14, 23, 24, 30, 51, 53, 55, and 71 by Luba Zagurak; on page 34 by Quinn McIlhone. All film photos from the private collection of V. Bryan; reprinted with permission.
Model appearing in "The Western Woman's Guide to Quebecois Men": Paul Duchaine
The publishers gratefully acknowledge the assistance of Paul Duchaine, Julien Duchaine, Michael Bailey, Gethin Stevens, and Patrick Johnson. Many thanks to all those who contributed to this venture.

Printed in Canada at John Deyell Company
Dépôt légal — quatrième trimestre 1985
Bibliothèque nationale du Québec

Eden Press
4626 St. Catherine Street W.
Montreal, Quebec
Eastern Canada   H3Z 1S3

TABLE of CONTENTS

THREE SOLITUDES

The *Random House Dictionary* defines *east* as "being in the end of the church where the high altar is." Nova Scotians could argue that their view of the altar isn't any better than Alberta's, despite being in the right end of the church. Quebecers have often complained that though they are close enough to see the fire, they are rarely close enough to feel its warmth. The East has always been a relative concept. To a Westerner it may mean Ottawa or Montreal. To a Torontonian it might mean Charlottetown or Taiwan, and to a Newfoundlander it could mean just about anything. The East is in fact three separate entities that possess a notion of eastness, but they do so with the natural suspicion of a child forced to share his toys with the neighbour's brat.

Ontario sits like a proud bowl of porridge on the western border, hoarding the small-town values that most people feared had skipped town when Dief left office. Ontarians pride themselves on their thrift, practical marriages, and on having the good sense to ban Magaret Laurence's books as the devil's instrument. At the hub lies Toronto, a melting pot that welcomes all people; Chinese, Greek, Italian, Jamaican and defensemen who can't skate.

Quebec has never been the type of province you would invite into your home. It makes too much noise, drinks till all hours, and doesn't know when to leave. For its part in Confederation it has supplied maple syrup, political drama, at least half of this country's hold-up men, and more Stanley Cups than you can shake a stick at. In Montreal, the tourist industry flourishes, but the general consensus of English Canadians seems to be that it is a better place to visit than to live in.

The Atlantic provinces are united by their relationship to the sea and the belief that they were the only provinces not given an opportunity to sleep with Margaret Trudeau. Their natural resentment towards upper Canadians has been tempered over the years by selling them lobster at $15.95 per pound, but a certain suspicion remains. While unemployment is still the biggest growth industry, there is this business of offshore oil and the truly frightening possiblity of Maritime oil barons.

Although often lumped together for the purposes of grade five geography books, the eastern provinces are in fact three solitudes.

Don Gillmor

EASTERN CANADA'S NEW CONSERVATIVE STYLE
by Elaine Edelstein

The label "eastern liberal" was one that enjoyed a certain vogue through the last two decades. The term "western liberal" failed to catch on, mostly due to the fact that there were only seven of them and they were referred to by name when the topic came up. An eastern liberal was more than someone who simply voted Liberal and worked for the CBC. An eastern liberal was sensitive to causes, though slightly squeamish around the actual issues, especially if they involved hunting seals or gelding anything. Unlike NDPers, who would march at the drop of a beret, eastern liberals preferred to put on tweed jackets and jeans and discuss the problem amongst themselves over a modest Bordeaux.

The husky voice of our stylish new PM, reminiscent of one most girls hear in the back of a Dodge with a hand resting on their knee, has seduced a nation that is just starting to look for its socks and ponder the consequences. For along with the tax breaks for small business and the increased commitment to NATO, we have voted for and will have to live with, the new conservative style.

THE OLD EASTERN CONSERVATIVE STYLE

It has been some time since the words *conservative style* haven't constituted a *non sequitur* when strung together. For years, conservative style

as it pertained to the East usually indicated a lack of any other kind or described the type of play a team adopted when they were thirty points ahead (a rarity for eastern teams). For the most part, the use of *conservative* as an adjective was limited to estimates and the Granite Club. Sedans, 60 percent other fibres, and sensible footwear were the extent of the conservative mystique. They were lauded for their common sense, mortgages they could afford and good seats at the Ice Capades.

An elusive concept, style requires not only a certain measure of creativity, but also, well, a sense of style. The rest of the East didn't much care whether conservatives had style or not. They made good neighbours, you could trust them with children, and so what if Jim wore black socks with his bermudas when he mowed the lawn? He wasn't really hurting anyone. And they did good charity work, if your definition of a charity was sufficiently flexible to admit the Rosedale Society for Reliable Fur Storage.

NOBODY EVER THOUGHT THEY WOULD COME TO POWER

After the Clark era, a chapter of Canadian politics so goofy one would think it would discourage further attempts, the Conservatives again subsided into the role they knew best, that of the grumpy Opposition. Brian Mulroney, however, successfully assaulted the seat of power with a style that

dazzled the old guard and attracted those eastern Liberals who weren't much on policy anyway.

Overnight, the conservatives went from being punctual and quick to lend gardening tools to arbiters of our political destiny. What was once the charm of matching Lacoste shirts on strolling couples suddenly took on the ominous suggestion of a uniform. On Bay Street, the men still dressed like pallbearers, but there was an air in their manner, a jauntiness in their step that had not been there before. No longer a foursome waiting to tee off in seven different plaids, the eastern conservatives now had style. Sort of.

The Ontario Conservative Party learned a hard lesson in style when they mistakenly ran old Conservative Frank Miller in the last election. Torontonians don't give a damn how retrograde their PCs are as long as they shop at the right stores. Provincial Conservatives demonstrated that they would rather have a Liberal as premier than a Conservative who once sold used cars and still dressed the part.

THE GETTING OF STYLE

The dovetailing of YUPPIE concerns with the eastern conservative putsch has forged a new style that has taken the insular stodginess of the old school and set it down squarely in the back seat of a BMW en route to taste the new Beaujolais. The new Ottawa conservative family no longer looks as if they just walked off the pages of a grade three reader; Dick and Jane have been replaced by a modest wine cellar that requires considerably less maintenance. "Conservative values," a term once reserved for concepts like pulling your own weight and regularly washing your Buick, have been stretched to embrace the merits of espresso makers and extra virgin olive oil.

CONSERVATIVE SEX APPEAL

What one finds attractive in the opposite sex has undergone a subtle shift in emphasis in eastern circles. Ottawa women who once adhered to *Cosmopolitan*'s listing of flat stomachs and nice bottoms as the two sexiest qualities in a man now lean towards "well groomed" and "a good credit rating." Certainly a diversified stock portfolio will go a long way towards making up for the absence of blue eyes and broad shoulders. Men, for their part, have forsaken qualities like "independent" and "good sense of humor" in favor of "good hostess" and "nonsmoker."

The eastern conservative is mostly interested in meaningful sex, that is, sex that will result in an MBA candidate. This is a revision of the eastern liberal's interpretation; they felt that any sex not involving farm animals held some meaning.

STRESS AND THE NEW ETHIC

Stress has become chic. If you don't suffer from it, either what you do isn't sufficiently important or you're not doing enough of it. Stress has become a question of status; the more you suffer, the more crucial your occupation. Once the exclusive province of air traffic controllers and brokers on the trading floor, it has trickled down to include shoppers approaching the limit on their Mastercard. When the going gets tough, the tough lunch at the Four Seasons.

I'M OK — YOU NEED A SAAB

One of the benefits of the new conservative style is the fact that it is no longer fashionable to be part of a consciousness-raising group or of any form of therapy that elicits embarrassing confessions in a crowded room. Getting in touch with oneself has taken a back seat to getting in touch with the right tax lawyer. The new eastern conservative has wisely concluded that there are few things that can't be cured with a Gold Card. Psychiatrists, with their personal questions and Freudian conjecture, are no match for the simple truth as spoken by a good stockbroker: "Sell at fourteen and a half."

This isn't to say that all is raspberry vinegar and Simon Chang out there. Behind the sophistication of the new conservative there are still backyards full of paunchy Don Mills Rotarians flipping burgers in aprons inscribed with "Try my foot-long hot dog." The eastern conservative may not want to acknowledge his living heritage, but he knows that without it he'd be no better than a liberal.

The essence of any style is knowing when to jump off the bandwagon. Give it three more years than unpack the Nehru jacket and climb aboard the soul train.

THE LANGUAGE OF THE NEW CONSERVATIVE

The new eastern conservatives have developed their own vernacular, replacing the outdated expressions of the past. We are now seeing business terms coming out of the boardroom and infesting street idiom with phrases like "fiscal restraint." Here are some other examples.

OLD LIBERAL	OLD CONSERVATIVE	NEW CONSERVATIVE
The government has no business in the bedrooms of the nation.	The government has no business in the boardrooms of the nation.	The government is open for business.
Get in touch with the people.	Get in touch with the right people.	Be the right people and get in touch with a good tax lawyer.
The common law family.	The nuclear family.	Families with first-strike capability.
Get back to the land.	Get back to business.	Get back to where you came from.
Let my people go.	Let my people profit.	They're not my people.
The strength of this nation is its people.	The strength of this nation is the people I went to school with.	The strength of this nation is the people of America.
Do your own thing.	Do the right thing.	Do the right thing before the neighbours do it.
And so begins a dialogue with the people of this country.	And so begins a dialogue with the people with money in this country.	And so begins a dialogue with the businessmen of America.
Everyone should have access to an education.	Everyone should have an uncle in senior management.	Everyone should have a father who's a Conservative MP.
We are entering a new age of prosperity.	We are *finally* entering a new age of prosperity.	The cupboard is bare.

TORONTO'S MOST EXCLUSIVE CLUBS
Things Peter C. Newman Never Told You
by Frederick Biro

Hidden deep in the bowels of Toronto's business and financial community are the exclusive clubs of Toronto. Behind thick walls, large wooden doors, old money and years of tradition, they lay barriered against women, the NDP, Easterners, Westerners, and the twentieth century.

The trick, of course, is to get inside. Prospective members must satisfy rigid criteria.

"Sir, your application is the saddest document I have ever seen. According to this form, you never finished grade six, you were on workman's compensation most of your life, you like country music, and you've marked your religion as Rastafarian. Now really. Name me one good reason why we should let you into our club."

"My uncle died in England and he left me four hundred million, U.S."

Once accepted there are certain rules one must strictly obey. Most clubs refuse to allow members to tan any darker than chunky peanut butter and will suspend those who have until they return to a normal pink.

Assuming you have joined a club or, more likely, blackmailed a member into inviting you to his, there are still a number of obstacles to be overcome. The first of these is actually finding the club, which hasn't

seen the need to advertise its presence with nameplates, posters in the sub-way or ads in *The Toronto Sun*. When you do find it remember to remove the antlers from the front grill of your car, as well as any old bumper stickers that say "Let the eastern bastards freeze in the dark" before pulling up to the door. Limousines with smoked glass are the preferred cars of the club, but anything costing over forty thousand will do. In a pinch, try a late model American car and tell the doorman it's rented.

To avoid controversy, wear a blue suit, blue tie, white shirt, dark socks (that match), dark shoes, and deodorant. Don't give in to that impulse to wear your favorite cowboy hat, boots or the diamond earring your girlfriend gave you.

Assuming your appearance meets with the doorman's approval, and your host still hasn't found those pictures you took of him playing bingo in the union hall, the heavy oak doors of the club should swing open as

you approach. As you enter, you will immediately sense that, much like Neil Armstrong, you have arrived in a different world.

In this world, the first scent to assail you is the smell of old cigars smoked by old men. Most club members enjoy a good cigar before the meal, during the meal, and after the meal, with the result that the dining room smells like a Cuban forest fire. The atmosphere aside, there are other traps in the dining room for the unwary guest. These include the delicate topics of conversation, table etiquette, and how to deal with the dining room staff.

It is probably safest to allow the members at your table to take the conversational lead while you study the number of utensils laid out before you. It will become immediately apparent that you have enough knives, forks and spoons to supply the Rotary Club's Annual Pancake Breakfast. In treading this labyrinth there are two rules of thumb. Watch the members at the table to see what they do, and if this fails always use the utensil from the outside first. However, if the serving staff insist on taking away the clean knife and fork after you have finished sawing your meat with the butter knife and dessert fork, don't argue. Use your napkin to clean them, or use your coffee spoon for dessert and drink your coffee black.

You should also observe the club members when it comes to dealing with the staff. Good staff are aware that they should serve and not be seen. Do not break this rule by saying thank you when a dish is removed or another course served. Not only will this embarrass your host, it will also blight the career of the staff person, who may seek retribution by pouring liqueur in your lap and then lighting it.

Scotch is the favorite club drink, rye is second, with water the preferred mix. If you absolutely abhor scotch and rye makes you get into fights, don't be reluctant to order something else. However, it is essential to avoid light beer, Canadian wine or anything non-alcoholic.

Unless you took drinking lessons from Ernest Hemingway, nurse your first drink. Don't attempt to follow the pace set by club members who regularly assault their kidneys with a fresh drink every fifteen minutes. Remember three things: most likely the members you are standing with will be chauffeured safely home; throwing up on the Persian carpet will dim your chances of being invited back; and if club members do ruin their kidneys, they can afford another one.

THE CLUBS

The Toronto Club ★ ★ ★ ½

The oldest and still most exclusive club in Toronto. The business club of the city, membership is limited to one person from any individual company and is usually the president or CEO. Total membership is also limited. Lost a half star when women were allowed entrance to certain areas in the evening.

The York Club ★ ★ ★

Considered the most stately of Toronto's clubs, the York also has limited membership. Unlike the Toronto Club, however, the York has a cross-section of members from business, cultural and artistic fields. This has resulted in the loss of a half star. The other half star was lost because of the York's lack of tradition as it was only established early in this century.

The University Club ★ ★

As its name indicates, a university degree is a prerequisite for joining this club. This resulted in the loss of a star as it is not possible to guarantee the political leanings of faculty members. Another star was lost as the club has a squash court, giving it some purpose.

The Ontario Club ★ ★

The Ontario Club lost a star when it was forced to relocate temporarily to an office tower after a fire. The second was lost as a result of the club's *laissez-faire* attitude, reflected in its recently considered move to admit female members.

The National Club ★ ½

Hit hard by the recession, the National allowed its membership to expand to include everyone who is anyone and their dog. Their sheer numbers have resulted in the loss of two and a half stars.

To be truly exclusive, a private club must exist only to create a world where no one but members may enter. Sports clubs, by the very duality of their purpose, immediately destroy this fragile environment. As soon as one begins to exercise, compete or sweat, a connection can be made to the great unwashed that lay on the other side of the heavy oak doors.

THE TORONTO MEDIA

The West, the Maritimes and Quebec have rarely reached a consensus on anything. Yet on one issue they stand united: The Toronto media is full of liberal pinheads who think the sun rises and sets in Peter Gzowski's booth. The rest of Canada has accused the Toronto media of being narrow, elitist, ill-informed and unwilling to look farther than Etobicoke for news.

Knowlton Nash, for example, ad libs the news from anywhere outside Toronto's downtown area, so the news from Calgary could be, depending on Knowlton's mood, ". . . while in Calgary tonight, country music remains popular despite the limitations of the genre," or ". . . in Calgary today, Mayor Ralph Klein admitted he wasn't too keen on having a 'bunch of foreign trash' in his city during the Olympics."

"The National" also never misses an opportunity to bring some Toronto relevance to any international story:

"The existence of God was verified today by Mount Palomar physicists . . . a spokesman for Bay Street denies the discovery will influence Monday's trading" (cut to stock footage of Bay Street).

"The Journal" no longer interviews western personalities due to an unfortunate incident with Peter Lougheed. When Mr. Lougheed's image came on Barbara Frum's screen, he began the discussion by saying, "You look cuter 'n a speckled pup in that frilly shirt, honey." Ms. Frum stipulated that a future condition of her staying with the show was that "the West" would henceforth refer to "Bloor Street West."

As part of it's national mandate, *The Globe and Mail* affords those in Carrot River, Saskatchewan, an opportunity to see a list of every item in The Art Shoppe's annual furniture sale. Similarly, sports fans in Pilot Mound, Manitoba, are grateful to know that Darling Carling Bassett is resting up after shooting another commercial with her father.

A. Roy Megarry points out to his detractors that the *Globe's* editorial policy has never been to report the news of the nation but rather to report the news of Toronto to the nation: "The *Globe* allows people everywhere to feel they are part of Toronto after they come in from milking the cows or whatever the hell it is that they do out there."

THE TORONTO STAR BESTSELLER LIST

NON-FICTION

1) SHOP YOUR WAY THROUGH MENOPAUSE, Dr. Muffy Anderson
2) HOW YOU CAN BENEFIT FROM THE COMING MONETARY COLLAPSE, Michael Wilson
3) THE NOUVELLE CHIEN COOKBOOK, Pierre duMerde
4) LEAD WITH YOUR CHIN, Brian Mulroney
5) MEIN KAMPF IN MEIN HARDHAT, Ernst Zundel
6) THE LAST SPIKE IN THE VALLEY OF THE GWANGI, Pierre Berton.
7) IT'S ALL GREEK TO ME; THE McCAIN FROZEN PIZZA COOKBOOK, Bruno Gerussi
8) THE ONE-MINUTE MANAGER, John Turner
9) THE FRONT PAGE CHALLENGE WORKOUT BOOK, Berton, Kennedy et al.
10) THE PALACE COUP, Rusty and Gerome

FICTION

1) Margaret Atwood's Newest Novel
2) Alice Munro's Latest Collection of Short Stories
3) Timothy Findley's New Book
4) Margaret Atwood's Last Book
5) Robertson Davies' Forthcoming Gothic Trilogy
6) Joseph Skvorecky's Recently Published Emigré Treatise
7) Gary Lauten's Next Pile of Newspaper Clippings, Winner of the Stephen Leacock Award
8) Leonard Cohen's Newest Book of Mournful Verse
9) Mavis Gallant's Incisive Collection of Short Fiction
10) Mordecai Richler's Long-Awaited New Novel

EASTERN CLASSIFIED ADS

LOST

A sense of purpose. If found please return to Liberal Party. Box 200, Ottawa. Sinecure offered.

A reason or reasons to gloat. Probably some time in February. Please return to PC Party. Box 201, Ottawa.

FOUND

A scapegoat for the Tory defeat in last Ontario election. Found near Muskoka area.

HELP WANTED

22 teenagers with interest in sports. Ability to skate preferred but not essential. Contact H. Ballard.

OPEN HOUSES

East Montreal. Seats 80,000. Ideal for entertaining. Needs some work. Contact J. Drapeau. Serious enquiries only.

POSITIONS WANTED

Handsome, tactile, executive type. Silver hair, blue eyes, an asset to any company. Looking for senior position in law firm. Willing to relocate. Contact J.T., Ottawa.

11,000 hardcore football fans looking for professional franchise to cheer for. Willing to relocate. Write c/o Ivor Wynne Stadium, Hamilton.

MUSICAL NEEDS

Soul, rhythm or blues influence needed by established MOR recording artist. Black people please apply. A. Murray, Nashville.

INVESTMENT PROPERTY FOR SALE

The prairie provinces and Atlantic provinces. Open spaces, great potential for development, ideal for American businessmen. All provinces fully serviced, some with view of the ocean. Willing to break up a set for right offer. Send bids to B. Mulroney, 24 Sussex Dr., Ottawa.

PERSONALS

Sincere bachelor, 40s, enjoys history, hardhats, walking in the rain and the company of Aryans, looking for discreet woman willing to share romantic dinners, Wagner and lunatic opinions. Ernie Z. Toronto.

FOR RENT

Cabbagetown studio apartment. Close to subway, dance class and people who understand brunch. $950.00 per month. 555-2911. Ask for Evian.

WANTED

A drink after 1 a.m., smoked meat, a hockey team, and a sense of *joie de vivre*. Contact the Montreal Resettlement Committee.

THE BEST INVESTMENT IS AN EXCLUSIVE EDUCATION

ATTENTION WEALTHY WESTERNERS

Oedipus College

Pecuniae omnes sunt

Will your son fail to have the advantages that only an exclusive education in the east can offer?
Will he fail to make those all-important contacts within the eastern establishment Old Boy network?
Then consider enrolling your son in the East's most exclusive school for the very, very rich.

Oedipus College

SCHOOL FOR BOYS

Over the years Oedipus College has established a reputation for excellence in schooling the sons of the Canadian elite. Our curriculum includes not only the basics of an elementary education but also offers a selection of courses geared to your child's unique position in society.

These include:

Exploiting the Masses   Bourgeois Baiting
Corporate Take Overs   Wealth: How to Flaunt It
Strike Breaking   Purchasing an NHL Franchise

DRESS CODE
School policy requires that students be clothed at all times.

BOOKS
Must be rented from the school in the original leather-bound edition engraved in gold foil.

TUITION
$250,000 (U.S.) per annum. There is an additional fee of $50,000 if your son fails to complete his year successfully; failure costs.

COMMENTS FROM SOME OF OUR WELL-KNOWN OLD BOYS
"Remove my name from your alumni mailing list immediately."
B. Mulroney
"My days at Oedipus made me what I am today."
C. Thatcher
"I am devoted to the boys at the junior school
for whom I can always spare some of my precious time."
C. Charon

HEADMASTER
Pugnacious Moron, B.A., M.A., Ph.D. (University of Toronto Bookroom)

For an expensive glossy brochure on our school that reiterates the above information, please contact the Headmaster, Oedipus College, Administration Block, The Only Place, Eastern Canada OLD BOY. Don't call us. We'll call you.

OEDIPUS COLLEGE SCHOOL FOR BOYS
(Accredited under the laws of nature.)

OTTAWA AT A GLANCE

by G. Arthur Sage

HISTORY: Ottawa was formerly known as Bytown since everyone in the area simply passed it by. In fact, only certain Indian tribes could ever find the place until Colonel By stumbled on the new capital, looking for construction materials for a canal he was building. Colonel By reported his discovery to Queen Victoria, who had been looking for a way to keep Canada a dull wasteland by excluding Montreal and Toronto as capitals. Ottawa was declared the capital, Queen Victoria died, and Ottawa followed suit.

GEOGRAPHY: Ottawa sits in a snow belt, thus confirming the foreign view of Canada as a land of ten-month winters broken up by two months of black flies. Rainfall is at the national average, with festivals running considerably above the national average.

POPULATION: Achievers in Ottawa tend to become politicians, LED executives (light-emitting device) or exotic wine-bar managers. Overachievers become doctors, taxi drivers and artists. Underachievers become civil servants.

Fitness and diet are preoccupations of the populace. When the rest of the country participated in "cola wars," Ottawa participated in the "bran fiber battles." Every morning after breakfast there is no water pressure in the city.

Sports are all the rage in Ottawa. People jostle to play squash with their lawyers, and body counts are high when designer tennis gear goes on sale. Windsurfing is popular because of the surfeit of wind.

POPULAR ATTRACTIONS: Ottawa is a showcase city that has developed rapidly with the infusion of money from across Canada. Among the exciting attractions are Parliament Hill, the Museum of Man and the fashions of years gone by worn by the citizens.

OTTAWA: Tory members react to charges of patronage from the Opposition.

To experience Ottawa as a native it is imperative to first avoid the Parliament Buildings. A single trip illustrates the fact that not only do the natives stay away in droves, so do the Honorable Members. On a good day MPs are vastly outnumbered by Japanese tourists who, with the help of a visiting grade four class, could take over the reins of government without a shot fired.

A NEW DAWN IN QUEBEC
Just Walk Away René
by Lynette Stokes

As most folks in western Canada have probably guessed, the people of Quebec were pretty much uplifted by Brian Mulroney's victory at the polls in 1984. But, when push comes to shove, what can you say about the political passions that animate a province that is just as happy to put a Tory in Sussex passions that animate a province that is just as happy to put a Tory on Sussex Drive as they are to put a separatist in their provincial assembly? The fact is that Quebec is nowhere near as inscrutable as people like to make out.

This overwhelmingly Catholic province feared no earthly retribution when it thumbed its nose at Ottawa in 1976, because they knew that there are only two influences that count: the church and the media. Catholicism has set Quebecers free, and the media has helped keep them there. After all, when you're distanced from mere local errors by a universal hierarchy, who cares about some petty constitution, right?

Catholicism has not only set Quebecers free, it has also made them positive. In other, more Protestant provinces, talk of separation would have led to endless discussions, with all sides dying of boredom, and the revolution would have blown over for good.

It is with a confidence born of conviction that Quebecers peer down the grim vista of the years ahead. *Que sera, sera.* Especially if it's entertaining, too. Only a Quebecer could elect a government on a separatist issue, and then refuse to give it a mandate to carry out its policies afterwards,

or tolerate an admission that porno movies have been filmed in the provincial legislature. In the speaker's chair, even. But Quebecers just shake their heads indulgently; their God may be a vengeful God, but he knows a good joke when he sees one.

Best of all, when Claude Charon, PQ speaker of the house, was caught red-handed shoplifting an English-style tweed jacket from Eaton, did he throw himself on the mercy of the law? No. He made a break for it, and had to be tackled in the snow on a crowded Montreal boulevard. "What has two coats but still runs?" joked the electorate, who burned their Eaton credit cards when the store decided to prosecute.

Well, they were heady days, but separatism is an idea whose time has come and gone. Quebecers are tired, and would be happy just to see the Canadiens winning in the play offs again.

Yet visitors to the province still half expect to see long-haired, drug-crazed, university students lusting for blood in the streets, while tumbrills rattle across the cobblestones of Old Montreal.

Visitors enjoy the carnival atmosphere of Montreal's historic Jacques Cartier Square.

These ill-informed people are merely victims of the media, who still labour under the delusion that the advent to power of the PQ constituted some kind of revolution. Levèsque, they never tired of telling us, was the victim of his own extremists, under whose influence the Parti Québecois was taking a sinister lurch to the left.

Take away the excitement of the all too easily excited media, and you'll discover that no one is much interested in the PQ any more. In fact, the media have not yet cottoned to the fact that what is of passionate interest to them is rarely of any interest to the general public. What keeps the separatism issue alive at all are the media pundits, who have been so immersed in "making disclosures" and "shedding light" on the state of the province, that they are not yet willing to take this tedious nonsense off the front pages.

An idea whose time has gone.

So, Quebec has mellowed out. Of course, polls are still taken regularly on the subject, and they show that most Quebecers are quite indifferent to the matter.

If truth be told, the last few years have been pre-eminently a time for half-measures in the political life of Quebec. Cynics even say that it has been a time for no measures at all. Hell, Montreal is only barely hanging on to it's title of bank-robbery capital of Canada, and there are people who claim to have seen signs of Protestantism creeping in amongst the work force.

But the times are changing. Is this, then, the end of an era? You bet. But it's not the one that non-Quebecers think of. That one ended years ago.

A new star has been seen in the East, and Quebecers are looking towards Ottawa with a new curiosity. The wind of change is blowing across the province, and the air has turned quite blue with epithets.

So, is Quebec ready to take up the torch of brotherhood at last? Could the interest that has been inspired by Ottawa spread even further west? Only the people of Quebec can decide. And that's what we're all afraid of.

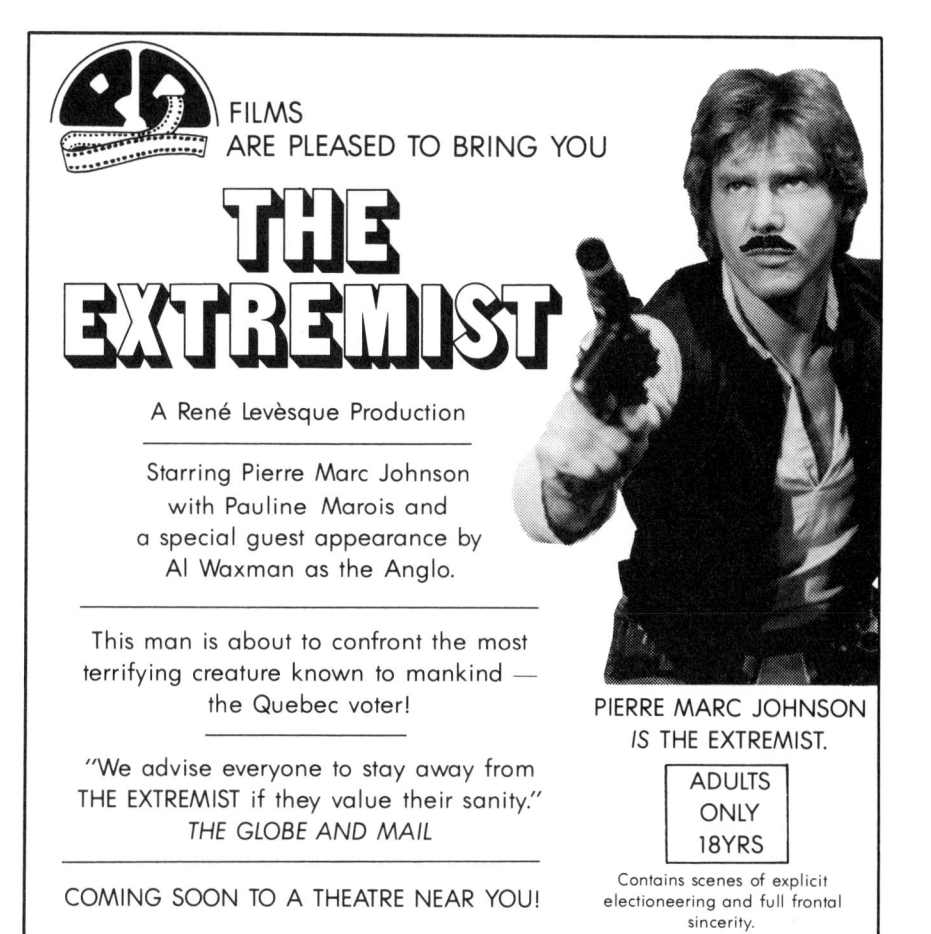

THE WESTERN WOMAN'S GUIDE TO QUEBECOIS MEN
by Emmanuelle Gattuso

Western women who visit Montreal in pursuit of the male of the species should beware of one thing: Montreal women. The competition is fierce, like nothing any western woman has ever experienced — except perhaps on "Ladies Night" at the Calgary Stampede. My advice: Take an empty suitcase, bring beaucoup de money to buy les fashions, and leave your jogging shoes at home.

Now about les males. Like the city, divided by Boulevard St-Laurent into east and west, so are the men. Follow this general rule. On the west side, you will meet the anglos and on the east side, the francophones.

Do not rule out the anglos. They are not your garden-variety English-speaking Canadian type unless, of course, they have just moved from Toronto (which is highly unlikely since most Toronto anglo men are intimidated by anything more cosmopolitan than cherry cokes atop the CN tower). Besides speaking your language and understanding most of it, the Montreal anglos differ from their Canadian counterparts in more ways than one. Two actually:

1. Montreal anglophones never wear white patent leather shoes with their plaid suits.
2. They can tell the difference between an English- and a French-speaking female from two kilometres away. (Some of them can even tell the difference between French and English wine.)

So, brush up on that English of yours, gals, and try to smile like Anne Murray — they may fool with Gigi, but they'll marry wholesome every time.

Getting to the body of the matter, les hommes, as we commonly complain about them, can be safely divided into the following categories:

The Post Referendum Séparatist

The Rich Vrai Québeçois

He is very emotional and will tell you all about his previous lovers and, of course, his politics. He will attempt to convince you that the PQ saved Quebec and the rest of Canada from the American plague. He will urge you to put all of your energy into working for the party, which, he is convinced, should be the only legitimate power in Quebec once independence is achieved. He is in a big hurry to change the world and this might not be a desirable trait in other types of activities, if you get my drift.

He will take you to restaurants where owners and waiters know him by name, bars where his favorite ("Comme d'habitude") drink is served as he walks in. He will openly talk about his divorce — a lawyer colleague represented him, a psychiatrist friend helped him through it, and his family trust fund paid for it. If this is your type, bring along a copy of your family tree and wear your family crest on your underwear. After all, his family has been in Quebec for twelve generations and they have spoken French and English since 1692; yours only got off the boat during the depression, unilingually Ukrainian.

The Nouveau YUPPIE

The Greaser

This man may have come from the east end, but he hasn't set foot there in many years. His nouveau accent is a cross between Portage La Prairie Manitoban and Jean Paul Belmondo. He wears nouveau designer jeans on weekends and has an upper, upper-level job. He reads *Le Devoir* and listens to Radio-Canada so he can contribute to the dinner conversation at his friends' elegant renovated town-houses. He will speak English to you in private, but not in the presence of his YUPPIE friends — it just isn't fashionable. (YUPPIE, pronounced You-pee, should not be confused with the Expos' mascot.) If you think you'd like color-coordinated sex, this man's for you.

If this man ever grew up, he could make a fortune publishing the first complete joual dictionary. He not only knows and uses every exsting joual word and expression, but he creates new ones as needed. His eclectic tastes run from hot-dog steamés to binnes en cannes (canned beans), from the comics in *Le Journal de Montreal* to the photographs in *Minuit* (trust me, you do not want to know more). For those of you who may not know, joual is to the French language what cockney is to the conservative English tongue. He thinks of women as "des calisses de beaux bébés" and has never looked one in the eyes. However, his sexual vocabulary alone may make the experience worthwhile.

A QUEBEC CONSPIRACY
THE TRUTH BEHIND NOUVELLE CUISINE

by Don Gillmor

Though nouvelle cuisine is no longer big news, it still occupies a lot of space on eastern menus. Part of its charm is the pairing of unlikely ingredients, producing a marriage of seemingly incompatible flavors that startle and refresh the palate. Liver and onions have given way to liver and peaches. Roast beef *au jus* is now beef in a green grape sauce. Pine nuts have crept into our consciousness like damp rot in the root cellar. Lighter and less calorically devastating than the cuisine of the saucier, it arrived in time to woo those who had just discovered jazzercising.

Purists may argue that other cultures have been mating unlikely foods for generations and that there is nothing nouvelle under the sun. It is true that the Moroccans have combined unmentionable camel parts with goat's eyes for a feisty stew for years and, closer to home, the English have paired blood with pudding. Even the Scots have linked watery eggs and dry toast with the notion of breakfast. But like a pop song without a good hook, these failed to reach a wide audience and have remained regional curiosities consumed well out of range of the golden arches.

Nouvelle cuisine reached an international market by insuring that at least one item in every dish was recognizable, and by banking on people's willingness to try anything if it is fashionable. The French have been credited with this creation and while they have marketed it succesfully, they did not in fact originate nouvelle cuisine.

The truth is that nouvelle cuisine was invented by the Kraft Food Corporation of Montreal.

In the fifties the Kraft Food Corp. began flogging its line on TV; cheddar cheese, mayonnaise. Nothing unusual here. Subsequent corporate growth dictated a diversification into miniature marshmallows, barbecue sauce, caramels, and finally to that no man's land between foodstuffs and chemistry: Velveeta, Sandwich Spread and Miracle Whip. It was correctly perceived by clever marketing strategists that sales would benefit substantially if recipes called for half a dozen or so Kraft products. They further realized that the combination of any six Kraft products would produce a bilious mess and the public would shun the idea if it were foisted upon them by slick Montreal marketing men. They hit upon the plan of introducing recipes from housewives from the hinterland and rewarding such resourcefulness and creativity with a modest stipend.

Thus on May 13, 1963, Kraft introduced a recipe submitted by a Mrs. Agatha Whelk of Departure Lake, Ontario.

DEPARTURE LAKE BOUILLABAISSE
3 fresh lake trout
1 lobster in season
1 lb. scallops
1 potato
6 large shrimp
2 small perch
1 cup Velveeta
2 cups Green Goddess salad dressing
1 bag Kraft caramels, wrappers removed
1 box Kraft Dinner
season to taste with Kraft miniature marshmallows.

The reassuring voice of Bruce Marsh recited the recipe while the camera panned the orgy of ingredients and finally focused on the shotgun marriage of flavors bubbling darkly in the Corningware dutch oven. On the black and white TVs around the country it looked like documentary footage of an offshore oil spill, but to the great surprise of the executives at Kraft, it was a hit. In a matter of days, over two hundred recipes were sent in from across the country, each more bizarre than the last. A perverse nerve had been struck in the repressed housewife population, and they responded with a vengeance.

The Kraft Revolution had begun. The dining rooms of the nation were soon littered with victims.

"What the hell are these little white spongy things in the pot roast, Dot?"

"It's something new I tried."

"You're goddam right it's something new."

The evolution of a great cuisine usually starts in the heartland, where there is limited availability of certain foods and the ingenuity of the locals is taxed to prepare potatoes every night without appearing redundant. When this ingenuity travels to the city it is revised with a cup of wine and given a title change by sophisticated chefs, allowing the urban populace to embrace it as its own.

The main reason the Kraft concept failed to achieve international status was its inability to garner acceptance from Canadian urban centres. The parade of recipes from Pelican Portage, Pickle Crow and Chibougamau were as suspect for their geographical origin as for the wanton mating of incongruous Kraft products. If Toronto gourmands thought Catherine Deneuve was eating apple crumble with barbecue sauce, you'd see it on every fork in Yorkville. It is another thing altogether when the suggestion comes from Mrs. Q. Kinacki of Neepawa.

A Canadian cuisine that was born in a fevered boardroom of Montreal and weaned in slow cookers from Nootka, B.C., to Cornerbrook, Newfoundland, failed to galvanize urban chefs into action. It was, perhaps, the greatest binding force in our nation, excluding the railway, yet we failed to recognize its true merit and left it to chill in the refrigerator of our collective memory. It took the French to realize the potential of this new cuisine. Paris was spinning its culinary wheels at the time and was searching for something new. Being Parisiennes, their search took the form of ignoring one another and consequently little was accomplished till recently. When the Kraft concept came to their attention they seized it, revised it and used their reputation as epicurean heavyweights to peddle the idea to the western world.

We have been usurped. And by the French. Mistrusting our cultural depth we have had our own invention sold back to us by a country that thinks Jerry Lewis is a genius. There is a lesson to be learned here: just because we thought of it and it was a terrible idea doesn't mean there isn't a fortune to be made from it.

HOW TO GET A JOB IN THE EAST

There was a time when vehicles full of Easterners cluttered the highways in search of western fortune. They sought careers in the wide-open economic spaces of the West, but many have returned, disillusioned, broke, or wanted by the Calgary police. For these people and for those Westerners who may want to seek employment in the East, here are some tips on landing the job of your choice.

HOW TO BE AN OTTAWA CIVIL SERVANT

1) When you're invited to a party, bring your Bob Newhart records and a jellied salad.
2) Stick to brown and beige co-ordinates in Banlon polyester. Experiment with sports coats that show four inches of shirt cuff or cover your knuckles.
3) Wear the ties your senile aunt has been sending you for Christmas every year.
4) Develop a smile that communicates the thought, "Not only will you not get a tax refund, you'll be lucky to stay out of jail."
5) Get your kid sister to cut your hair with her Romper Room safety scissors.
6) Practise living in a city for seven years not knowing where a good bar is.
7) Get a monthly transit pass and start saving for a small brown sedan.

HOW TO BE A TORONTO ACTOR

1) Wear a lot of black.
2) Use famous lines regularly in conversation: "Now is the winter of our discontent," "I coulda been a contendah," etc.
3) Tell everyone that eventually you'd like to direct.
4) Get a job in a restaurant.
5) Memorize the specials of the day.
6) Be able to recommend an appropriate wine.
7) Learn to recognize who is paying and cater to them.
8) Know your desserts.

HOW TO BE A NEW BRUNSWICK POLITICIAN

1) Score some good Columbian.
2) Familiarize yourself with Montreal.
3) Familiarize yourself with Richard Nixon's political career.

HOW TO BE A MONTREAL CAB DRIVER

1) Watch *Bullitt* sixteen times.
2) Learn to understand English only after there are twenty dollars on the meter.
3) Learn to judge to what degree a light is red.
4) Develop the habit of lighting one Export A after another.
5) Develop a disdain for human life as it applies to pedestrians.
6) Learn the secret meaning of *arrêt*.

HOW TO BE A QUEBEC NORDIQUE

1) Start reading the cereal box from the other side.
2) Fight regularly with Mario Tremblay. Knock on his door and fight him in his living room if it's summer.
3) Have your front teeth pulled.
4) Practise sitting by yourself for two minutes at a time.
5) Memorize this phrase, "Well, Bill, h'ah t'ink we jus' play dat fundamental 'ockey, eh?"

HOW TO BECOME A MEMBER OF THE NATIONAL BALLET OF CANADA

1) Start walking duckfooted.
2) Get used to smoking instead of eating.
3) Do stretching exercises in the bank lineup.
4) Don't participate in any conversation that doesn't focus on your body.

HOW TO BE AN OFFSHORE NEWFOUNDLAND OIL RIGGER

1) Buy a bumper sticker for your truck that says "Let the western bastards drown in their own oil."
2) On your application form, state that you are a relative of John Crosbie's or a close personal friend of either of his two sons.
3) Learn how to spend all the money you made in the last three weeks in a forty-eight hour binge in St. John's.
4) Become a world-class swimmer.

HOW TO BE A CBC WRITER

1) Have a job as a mail clerk and get a promotion.
2) Set all your scripts in remote wilderness areas in the past.
3) Have a man character and a woman character but let the land (symbolically) do most of the talking.
4) Refuse to write anything but stark, brooding dramas. If you're assigned to "Fraggle Rock," have Wembley go up to a hunting lodge and shoot himself.

WHAT'S ON IN NOVA SCOTIA

THEATRE

Captain Highliner
presents
Codpiece Theatre
featuring Donald Sutherland
in

The Ancient Maritimer

with a special cameo appearance
by John Buchanan
as the albatross
Saturday — The Historic Properties
Halifax

The Truro Open-Air Operatic Society
bring you

The Pirates of Petro~Can

a fun-loving bunch of oil riggers
drink and loot their way around
the Nova Scotia coastline

DANCE

The Digby Clam Shuckers Society
Square Dancing Troupe
reinterpret Virginia Woolf's

To The Lighthouse

in traditional dance

ART

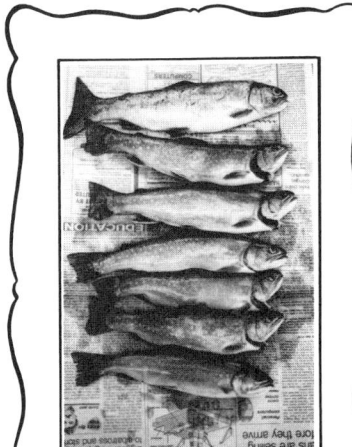

Self Portrait
by the Atlantic Group of Seven.
Peggy's Cove Museum of Modern Art

KENTVILLE CINEMA

FILM

RCMP ACADEMY

(Halifax Odeon)
Rookies patrol the
Trans-Canada highway
with zany results

LAWRENCE OF ACADIA

starring Peter O'Toole

A crazed Arab explores for oil in the Annapolis Valley

SINGLES BINGO

every night in Dartmouth church halls

MUSIC

The Reggae Symphony Orchestra
of Halifax play
a musical interpretation of
Shakespeare's classic

For he's a jolly good Othello

The JOE CLARK Five

mime to their latest recording at
Liverpool's Cavern Club

all week

DISCOVERING NEWFOUNDLAND
by Debra Reid

If you're planning a European trip but are short of money you might consider Canada's closest European point: Newfoundland. Europe and Newfoundland have many things in common, physically and spiritually. There are many theories as to the geographic origins of Newfoundland. The most popular of these is that Newfoundland was once attached to Ireland, but the two countries broke apart after a large shipment of rum blew up in the north Atlantic.

This explains the two most important elements of Newfoundland society. They still speak Gaelic and, like the Irish, are too stubborn to give up rum even though it caused the break with the homeland. After all, the Irish are accustomed to liquor breaking up the home.

There are two ways of going to Newfoundland — by ferry or by plane. If travelling by ferry in the winter, you should give yourself extra time because the ferry has been known to get stuck in the ice for weeks. This is partly due to the ice and partly due to the fact that the bar is free on a stuck ferry. The captain sometimes doesn't notice winter is over until the ice in his drink starts to melt.

Flying to Newfoundland also requires an adventurous spirit. Eastern Provincial Airlines is definitely the preferred airline. Six EPA flights will land in St. John's in the time it takes one Air Canada flight to bus its passengers from Gander to St. John's. Because of their ability to fly in the fog, the EPA pilots are stealing the pea-souper title from their neighbours in Quebec.

It is not difficult to choose a hotel in Newfoundland as there is usually only one hotel room left in the city. This is because most travellers to Newfoundland have been fogged in for much of their adult lives. In hotel lobbies you will meet travelling salesmen who are hoping to be assimilated into Newfoundland culture, and in three generations there is a good chance that Newfoundlanders will stop calling them mainlanders.

A break in the fog reveals Cornerbrook's bustling downtown core.

It is difficult not to be taken as a tourist, and your attempts to blend in will be shattered when you open your mouth. You could try carrying the *Dictionary of Newfoundland English* with you. Unfortunately, this phrasebook (the only one available) is hardcover and is difficult to slip into your purse or back pocket. One way around the language problem is by prefixing all your adjectives with "some" (some windy, some good, some phony). This will at least give you the chance of passing yourself off as a Maritimer, which is one step above the rest of Canada in the eyes of Newfoundlanders.

Newfoundlanders regard tourists in much the same way that most European countries do. They are happy to see you, they are happy to show you hospitality, they are happy to take your money, but they are happy to see you go.

A PRINCE EDWARD ISLAND TRAVELOGUE

 **YOUR ISLAND IN THE SUN** A summer vacation in P.E.I. offers the ultimate in safety in numbers because tourists outnumber natives four to one. Of course, this means that eighty percent of the people you meet there will be from New Jersey or Quebec. (Native Islanders are so rare that the Museum of Man would appreciate reports of any sightings.)

It's claimed that the majority of Islanders are potato farmers, and the endless acres of well-manicured fields do give that impression. Rumor also has it that because of the rolling hills of the Island, P.E.I. farmers have sea legs, but they are so rarely seen that this has yet to be confirmed.

Local farmers whoop it up during the Spud Festival at the Lucy Maud Community Centre.

Although Micmac Indian legends were invented to explain the dark red earth of P.E.I., the western visitor will quickly determine that the color is the result of the blood, sweat and tears that generations of tourists have poured into the Island in an effort to find a drink. In a province that enforced Prohibition from 1906 until 1948, alcohol can only be served by someone capable of doing so with a stern, warning glance.

The only non-red soil on P.E.I. is found along the white beaches. Swimming is relatively safe here — except for overweight tourists. Mistaking their beached bodies for whales, zealous Greenpeacers have been known to drag hapless sunbathers out to sea in a misguided attempt to save their lives.

Most visitors to P.E.I. either camp or stay at a farm that offers bed-and -breakfast. Many Westerners will find the latter option too much like home; they'll pitch in with the chores instead of visiting Ann of Green Gables's Dream House. Camping is generally a civilized affair on the Island. Tourists need not fear being mauled by a bear because there are no bears. In fact, as far as wildlife is concerned, you probably won't see anything bigger than a chipmunk. Campgrounds tend to be about as hard to live in as five-star hotels. For those who really want to rough it, the national and provincial parks are recommended as they don't have any tennis courts or satellite dishes.

YOUR ISLAND IN THE SNOW   Other Canadians may have Hawaii and Florida, but Maritimers have "The Island." There is no need for them to winter in the south when they have P.E.I. on their doorstep.

The Island is lovely in the summer with its rolling hills, rolling sand and rolling Winnebagos. However, the wintertime is the best time to come to the Island to really escape the tourists and enjoy this quiet seaside resort. The considerate Islanders also leave P.E.I. at this time to leave more room for this new type of tourist that is flocking to their snow-covered beaches.

The best method of transport is the CN ferry from Cape Tormentine, N.B., to Borden. The preferred departure time is early on a weekday. This insures that the ferry is occupied solely by truckers, and they're a lively, fun bunch of guys at seven in the morning. Chances are you'll get stuck in the ice and really get to know them well. There is a lot to do on a CN ferry for six hours: you can play the pinball machines, drink, eat, drink, nap, drink, and go to the washroom.

Upon arriving don't be surprised if P.E.I. looks a little bleak. There will either be no snow or a major snowstorm that will close everything down. This will allow you to spend extra time while the province's four snowploughs work their way around the Island. Meanwhile, you could take a walk on the snow covered dunes, drink, talk to the five natives that are left, sunbathe under the heat lamp in your hotel room, and drink. So, don't delay your trip any longer.

THE CARE AND EATING OF ATLANTIC LOBSTER

by David Miller

Many people know nothing of lobster. Reasons abound, but research shows that many people are put off lobster because they are ugly and there is no zipper to get at the meat. However, lobster is important in the economy of the Atlantic provinces both as a food (although they are well behind hot turkey sandwiches) and as a valuable export.

The lobster lives deep in the Atlantic ocean under rocks, old tires, empties, and discarded Chevies, and eats almost anything, including other lobster. They vary in size, from one pound to twenty pounds, although most East Coasters eschew the big ones as being tough and bearing too great a resemblance to the Hon. John Crosbie.

The color of lobster varies from light green to dark green, depending on the age and depth of the Chevy, till you cook them. Most East Coasters have no idea that lobster are members of the crustacea class and *Homarus senus*. Most firmly believe that lobster are members of the Lion's Club because they appear at so many suppers.

FROM DEEP TO PLATE

Travelling through the Atlantic region you will see few lobster in their natural habitat, but many on plates. Instrumental in this transition are the lobster fishermen, who everyone agrees are a hardy breed (check all periodicals, magazines, television, newspaper and radio treatment of them). To catch lobster, fishermen use traps or pots — odd looking things that cost from $1.50 to $1,000 — depending on whether you're a fisherman or a tourist.

Traps are baited with such things as herring and Spam before they are thrown off the boat.

The day after throwing the traps off the boat, the hardy fisherman goes back to "pull" them. This is not so tough, as most boats are equipped with automatic haulers. The fishermen have kept this a secret, in an effort to preserve their robust reputation for future *National Geographic* features.

When all his traps are pulled, the fisherman sails to the wharf where he fights for six hours with the buyer over price. Actually no one sails anymore, preferring to power their boats with 365 hp straight-eight Chrysler engines instead.

Eventually the buyer pays $3 and then sells them to retailers for $5, who in turn sell them to you for $29.95 — salad extra. Next, the lobster are put in trucks and driven to Boston, Toronto, Winnipeg, and Edmonton. For these trips it is customary to give the lobster valium to keep its crustacean neuroses under control. Certain western restaurants charge extra for this.

COOKING LOBSTER

There are many ways to cook lobster, but East Coasters only have two recipes: boiling and steaming. First a large pot is filled with water. Sea water is best because it is plentiful and no one has found anything better to do with it. If you're clear out of sea water, use plain water, salt, and sea shanties.

Put the lobster in the pot and place a cover on it. Wait until the cover starts to jump up and down. This indicates that the pot is boiling or that the lobster is still alive and trying to get out to seek revenge on you and your family. Give it twenty minutes in the boiling water or half a case of Schooner beer. When cooked, remove the lobster from the stove and douse with cold water.

EATING THE LOBSTER: THE PERILOUS PART

Cooked lobster looks delicious when it is on the plate, but there are a lot of inedible parts, and actually you'll be hungry in four or five minutes unless you have a lot of bread, beer, etc., to go with it. Do *not* eat the black stuff on top of the tail because this is the bowel and it is not highly prized. Remove the bowel and examine the tail. Prod it with a fork and lift it into the air. Say things like "Aaaaah, the tail." People will be impressed, especially those on bus tours.

After you eat the tail and claws you are finished. Some people poke around the body for an hour or so, but this is highly over-rated. Some also suck bits of meat out of the legs, but this is time consuming as a lobster has thinner legs than a French model and considerably more of them.

WHERE TO BUY LOBSTER, FRESH OR COOKED AND SOME PLACES TO EAT THEM

Don't buy lobster from the hardy fishermen because they will try to sell them to you for $9 per pound wrapped in old newspaper. Instead, go to a vendor who will supply boxes to properly transport the beasts. Pay no more than five dollars per pound and always check to see that they are alive. One method of doing this is to stick your finger in the box, but this is only recommended if you are lightning quick. Better to use a stick or tire iron.

If you don't want to cook your own lobster, look for a service club. All service clubs in the Atlantic Provinces (Lion's, Kiwanis, Kinsmen, Rotary, Sons of the Pioneers) have lobster dinners. A full dinner, including biscuits,

is in the $10 range, and the halls are always licensed, more for the staff's benefit than yours, but still handy. An Atlantic lobster dinner consists of a cooked beast, generally cracked (depending upon the sobriety of the staff), week-old potato salad, hard biscuits, paper plates, and strawberry shortcake.

Lobster are plentiful, chiefly because the average East Coaster doesn't eat lobster. They are too expensive and not nearly as good as a hot turkey sandwich.

A NEWFOUNDLAND DIARY

Monday

Johnny, me mate, proves again he is a scroopy[1] slinger[2] with little in his sou'wester[3] but figgy pudding.[4]

Still, he is me mate.

Tuesday

"Stog[5] yourself." I say to Johnny after his morning idiocy. (Today he tells me the government is full of smeachy[6] spurwinks[7] without the brains to make salt-water soup and he is going to be premier himself.)

He tells me he's smitten by the love plague. He thinks her name is Sheila.

Wednesday

Today we talk on his new love though he knows no more of love than a flang-tile.[8]

"Johnny." says I.

"Aye." says Johnny.

"Have you spoken with your betrothed, you nunny-fudging[9] bay noddy."[10]

"No." says he, thick with thought.

"How do you know she ain't some path walloper?"[11] I ask.

"Oh no." he says, "She is an angel descended and a dream come true."

I tell Peggy she is lucky not to be married to a scrumpy[12] soaker[13] like Johnny.

Thursday

Johnny broods that she is a bay-girl[14] and will spurn him sure, as that is their way.

I say "Quiff[15] yourself so she don't see you as some harbour tom-cod.[16] Dress like a buckaloon[17] and you'll be treated as a buckaloon. That's how I landed me Peggy."

I tell Peggy this at supper (berry duff[18] for dessert, would rather eat dirt) and she says I am a fountain of knowledge.

Friday

We go to Finney's Pub, ugly drung[19] of bay noddies, but three

Screeches and I don't mind the looks of them too much. Sheila is no prize I decide, but I keep me views to meself as she seems to like Johnny; no small feat. She asks him to dance and he queaks[20] yes and they are jigging about like flayed squid the rest of the night. Am drinking Screech like a pirate and have some difficulty finding my house. Peggy not happy to see me and gives me uncourteous greeting with a wooden spoon.

Saturday

Peggy treating me like a nuzzle-tripe[21] and threatening to poison my flang-tile. I slink into the fog, thinking all is not well on the rock.

Sunday

Johnny is behaving like a man with flipper pie[22] in his head. Must listen to his scroopy cries of love all day. He whistles like some gatching[23] buckaloon and gushes like a spawning lobster. I pray some great squid pulls him into the drink.

I tell Peggy that Johnny has no more brains than a cod-cake and is caught in the net of this bay-girl.

Peggy tells me to finish me berry duff.

1. *scroopy:* squeaky
2. *slinger:* idler
3. *sou'wester:* waterproof hat favored by fishermen
4. *figgy pudding:* plum pudding
5. *stog:* to block or clog an aperture
6. *smeachy:* unpleasant in taste and smell
7. *spurwinks:* a kind of seabird
8. *flang-tile:* a type of pancake
9. *nunny-fudging:* idling, shirking
10. *bay noddy:* mildly derogatory term for an inhabitant of an outport
11. *path walloper:* a woman who is seen frequently walking along roads with different followers, so to speak
12. *scrumpy:* overbaked
13. *soaker:* a very large trout
14. *bay-girl:* young woman of the outports
15. *quiff:* smartly got up, carefully dressed
16. *harbour tom-cod:* small immature cod-fish
17. *buckaloon:* man of some importance
18. *berry duff:* boiled pudding with berries
19. *drung:* crowd
20. *queaks:* a slight sound or squeak
21. *nuzzle-tripe:* misbehaving child
22. *flipper pie:* pie made from seal flippers
23. *gatching:* boastful

MONTREAL
The Festival Capital
by Debra Reid

Travellers to Montreal should always check on the city's "festivals." Montrealers have a fondness bordering on mania for festivals of every kind. As a result, the city hosts everything from Le Festival des Films du Monde (The Montreal World Film Festival) to Le Festival du Hot Dog Steamé (The Steamed Hot Dog Festival).

It is difficult to understand this festival madness. It can perhaps be explained by Montrealers' need to turn everything into an "event" for celebration.

The important thing is that it gives the natives an opportunity to get "decked out" in the latest fashion. This is no small feat in a city where you wear your Vittadini casual wear to go to the corner store. For the visitor to Montreal, put on your most outrageous outfit and enjoy. Here is a guide to the city's festivals — the famous and the not so famous ones.

CULTURAL FESTIVALS

THE MONTREAL WORLD FILM FESTIVAL: The film festival is an extravaganza for the film afficianado. This festival has earned the reputation of being the only film festival where the fans are more interested in the films than in the celebrities. This bizarre quirk makes star gazing much easier for visitors to the city. A day spent in the elevator of the Hotel Meridien should allow you to pass the time of day with Jane Fonda or Clint Eastwood.

THE MONTREAL INTERNATIONAL JAZZ FESTIVAL: The jazz festival is quickly becoming one of the world's "hot" jazz festivals, partly because of standard July temperatures (33°C). The steaming crowds take over St. Denis St., and if you're claustrophobic or prone to heat stroke, find another festival.

LE FESTIVALE INTERNATIONALE DE LA DANSE and LE FESTIVAL INTERNATIONALE DE LA NOUVELLE DANSE: As Montrealers' favourite recreation is dancing it comes as no suprise that the city needs two dance festivals to satisfy its body-conscious inhabitants. If you don't dance in Montreal it's because you're over eighty and have severe arthritis.

FOOD FESTIVALS

Everytime a new fruit or vegetable pops out of the ground some small Quebec town decides to hold a festival. In the coming years look for more festivals currently under consideration by the Ministry of Tourism (Le Festival de la Carotte, Le Festival du Broccoli, Le Festival de la Tomate). The Quebec Ministry of Tourism feels that if you've got vegetables, flaunt them.

Of all the Montreal festival organizers the ones that must be given credit for being the most imaginative are the city's restaurants, taverns and brasseries. (A brasserie is a tavern that has been re-decorated to appeal to women as well as men. *Brasserie* is a word chosen by French Canadians to confuse their English counterparts in the hopes that they will mistake it for a lingerie store.)

The restaurant festival trend started on a very reasonable note with Le Festival du Homard (The Lobster Festival). Every year the restaurant owners dig out their banners announcing Le Festival du Homard: Three Lobsters for Ten Dollars, and everyone knows that the lobster season is upon them.

The lobster festival was so successful that enterprising restaurateurs started to look around for other items that might lend themselves to festivalization.

Taverne Henri Richard announced Le Festival de la Salade. A St. Laurent St. restaurant hung out a banner for Le Festival du Hot Dog Steamé. A banner was spotted in east-end Montreal for Le Festival du Porc et des Fêves au Lard (The Pork and Beans Festival), and a downtown eatery put up a sign for its Festival du Club Sandwich.

It's difficult to say how far the restaurants will go. If it spreads to the city's French restaurants we can look forward to Le Festival du Café au Lait (The Coffee with Milk Festival).

Montrealers feel that food is a celebration and they're out to show the world that a simple *menu du jour* is not enough. "Today's Special" is a cause for festivity. People no longer want to "just" go to lunch when they can go to a festival.

EASTERN HUNTING REGULATIONS

Every year thousands of hunters come to the East's bountiful wilderness areas. Forests are teeming with big game (black bear, moose, deer, noisy teenagers on drugs) medium game (other hunter's dogs, farm animals) and small game (squirrels, foxes, Hammy Hamster, Peter Cottontail, Eeyore, Piglet, Pooh). If you come to hunt, remember, hunting is more than a bloodsport, it is a responsibility.

GUNS: Get close, kill clean. Legal weapons include hollowpoint rimfire handguns (Ruger's Mark 2 Target, Smith and Wesson

Hunting the ring-necked mallard in northern Quebec.

Combat Masterpiece, Colt .38, Quick-Draw MacGraw Autograph series) and fully automatic assault rifles (Uzi 9 mm., AK-47, Huot .303 Light Machine Gun).

DOGS: Sighthounds are allowed in most wilderness units if accompanied by Stud Book. Dogs should demonstrate less brindle than Dandie Dinmont Terriers but more than a Finnish Spitz. Point dogs should be prepared to give tongue (at least as much as a Karelian Bear Dog, but no more than a Cardigan Welsh Corgi). Flushounds should perform in the tradition of Kelpie, Puli's, Pugs and Soft Coated Wheaten Terriers, and should be in many ways, more than a wife.

ENDANGERED SPECIES: It is against wilderness protection laws to hunt Boat-Tailed Grackles, Red-Backed Voles, Kirtland's Warblers, White-Bellied Sand Rats, Salt-Marsh Grain Hens, Federal Liberals, Small-Tailed Fruit Skinks, Thompson's Blue-Haired Titmice or Ring-Necked Swamp Pigs.

Remember the hunters' code: The drunken hunters walk ahead of the more sober hunters. If all of you are falling down drunk, don't leave the motel room, shoot the television set and buy a deer at a roadside stand on the way home. Better to be safe than a statistic. Happy Hunting.

YOUR PRIME TIME
ENTERTAINMENT GUIDE
by Mike Boone

On any trip to the East, whether it be Toronto, Montreal or Drummondville, there comes a point in the day when the experienced traveller says, "I'm going back to the hotel to watch TV." This is an indication of what is to be found there.

PRIME TIME LISTINGS

6:00 p.m.
CBC LOCAL NEWS with an anchorman wearing horn rim glasses and a food-stained green tie, a weather girl with a moustache and a 63-year-old sports reporter who doesn't realize the NHL has expanded.
FC MOVIE — Comedy
Porky's (Canada, 1982) 2 hrs.
CTV LOCAL NEWS with a blow-dried pretty-boy anchorman who doesn't understand what he's reading off the teleprompter, a weather girl with huge breasts who makes jokes about blizzards, and a sports reporter in a maroon jacket who narrates an 8-minute film clip of hockey fights.
24 MacNEIL-LEHRER
Two incredibly boring guys interview Washington insiders who are even duller than they are.
26 McBOINGBOING-SCHNORER
Two tweedy Torontonians who make MacNeil-Lehrer look like Dean Martin and Jerry Lewis, interview the Ottawa and Queens Park insiders who are either too dull, too stupid or too ugly to appear on "The Journal."

7:00
8 KING OF KENSINGTON
Larry King (Al Waxman) shops for underwear at Zellers.

7:30
6 LORNE GREENE'S NEW WILDERNESS
Deep in the Australian outback, rodents shaped like tennis balls fight a valiant battle for survival against predators from the Davis Cup team.

8:00
6 THRILL OF A LIFETIME
A transvestite from Hamilton takes a shift on the Edmonton Oilers' power play; a Toronto banker has his toes sucked by a Trois-Rivières stripper; Conservative MP Robert Coates visits Hamburg, and Lloyd Robertson leaves home without any makeup on.
8 THE FIFTH ESTATE
Bob McKeown reveals that most people who buy lottery tickets don't win any money. Eric Malling tears the lid off chain letters. Hana Gartner exposes a mail-order aphrodisiac ring.

24 GREAT PERFORMANCES
The Black Shakespearian Theatre of Halifax performs *As You Likes It.*

26 REALITIES
Robert Fulford plays gin rummy with Lister Sinclair while Morley Callaghan kibbitzes and Richard Gwyn bakes fudge.

FC MOVIE — Drama
Porky's II (Canada, 1983) 2 hrs.

9:00
4 THAT'S INCREDIBLE
This week, two men from Chicoutimi, Quebec, who have jobs and don't drink, a Toronto lawyer who has never played tennis, and a Canadian Post Office employee who has gone two weeks without booking off sick.

6 MAPLE LEAF SHOWCASE
CTV launches a new series of Canadian dramas with "Night Patrol." Two Mounties (Telly Savalas and Lou Gossett Jr.) pursue the trail of a heroin trafficker (Cesar Romero) and corner their quarry by enlisting the aid of his illegitimate daughter (Jamie Lee Curtis), a ski instructor at Banff. Director: Brian De Palma. Based on a letter to the editor in *The Toronto Sun.*

8 THE NATURE OF THINGS
Using computer-directed micro-cameras, Dr. David Suzuki probes the deepest, darkest recesses of Prime Minister Brian Mulroney, culminating in a visit with political journalist L. Ian Macdonald.

MM CANADIAN VIDEO HOUR
New videos from Corey Hart, Parachute Club, Rough Trade, Doug and the Slugs and the Orford String Quartet.

12 LIVE IT UP
Jack McGaw visits a McDonald's in Thunder Bay. Alan Edmonds drives a Honda Civic in reverse from Calgary to Edmonton. Liz Grogan reports on a group of Don Mills housewives who have found novel applications for pogo sticks.

8 THE NATIONAL
FC MOVIE — Documentary
Porky's III (Canada, 1984) 2 hrs.

10:25
8 THE JOURNAL
Tonight, a documentary report on teenage girls who hang around the CBC's Toronto studios trying to catch a glimpse of Keith Morrison. Also, Tom Alderman takes a lighthearted look at drug use by sports commentators.

10:30
6 SNOW JOB
High times at the ski lodge when a visiting television network executive (Murray Chercover) offers to cast the staff in a TV series produced to satisfy Canadian content requirements. Courtney: Jack Creley, Camille: Pauline Julien, Biff: Wayne Gretzky.

NEW SHOWS
FOR THE UPCOMING SEASON

★ CBC will introduce "Capital Crime," a detective drama based in Ottawa that will feature Guy Lafleur as a private eye who cruises the frozen canals of the capital in the interests of justice. Karen Magnuson guest stars in the opening episode as a sociopathic figure skater out to avenge her perennially low scores at the hands of East German judges.

★ The comedy hit of the season may turn out to be CTV's "All About Yves," the hilarious adventures of a Montreal fashion designer who is accidentally transported by a time machine to the Paleozoic Age. Cultures collide in this comedy of manners with a twist.

★ This season, the first Canadian-American sitcom will hit the screen, a co-production of CTV and CBS. Joe Clark will star as a bumbling ex-prime minister who moves in next door to a bumbling ex-president (Gerald Ford) in a predominantly ethnic neighbourhood. Racial gaffs and slapstick unite in this riotous tour de farce to be titled "When Worlds Collide."

★ CITY-TV will present the Keith Richards Exercise Hour in the new season. The svelte Rolling Stone will demonstrate the exercises that have kept him slim through twenty years of rock 'n' roll and pass on the diet tips that have helped him keep his figure. In the season opener, Keith examines the three basic food groups; benzedrine (how much is too much?), heroin (addiction or breakfast?), and Jack Daniels (nature's perfect food?).

★ CBC is hoping for a hit with "Do Not Go Gentle" in which Dan Hill stars as a gay Toronto cop who lives with a moderately successful, though decidedly minor, feminist poet (Flora MacDonald) in a Mississauga trailer court. Inborn prejudices and sexual politics provide the sparks in this taut suburban drama.

★ Global TV will make a bid with the special "Whole Lotta Love." In this moving salute to Led Zeppelin, hosts Anne Murray and Julio Iglesias take us on a musical trip through the songs that virtually defined the genre of heavy metal. Guests stars include Al Waxman, Gilbert O'Sullivan and Topo Gigio, the Italian mouse.

★ In CBC's "Bubba for the Defence," a former football star (Rompin' Ronnie Hawkins) is expelled from the CFL on an exaggerated drug charge and sells his talents to Canada's defence effort. Barbara Frum stars as his boss, the tough but tender commander who still has something to prove.

★ Global hopes to hit big with a mini-series that combines mystery and fitness from two bestsellers; *Barbie Allen's Exercise Book* and John LeCarré's *Smiley's People.* Charles Nelson Reilly will star as the chubby British spy who wants to get into shape before he retires. Richard Chamberlain plays the Russian who infiltrates his health club, with Loni Anderson as the Czech gymnast in 'Tinker, Tailor, Soldier, Sauna."

★ In the CBC comedy "I Like the Nightlife" Richard Hatfield stars as a successful corporate lawyer who works as a waiter in a suspect after hours disco. Erik Nielsen plays his old army buddy Ernie.

A WESTERNERS' GUIDE TO EASTERN EQUIVALENTS

WEST	EAST
Bryan Adams	Corey Hart
James Keegstra	Ernst Zundel
Mel Hurtig	Jack McClelland
Jack Webster	Morton Shulman
The Heritage Fund	The Reichmanns
Wayne Gretzky	God
The West Edmonton Mall	The Great Antonio
The Calgary Stampede	The new Beaujolais
Oil money	Old money
16-ounce T-bones	Sushi
Winter	Florida
Louis Riel	Louis Riel
Peter Pocklington	Peter Worthington
Jack Horner	Eugene Whelan
Peter Lougheed	Prince Philip
Pickup trucks	BMWs
Shovelling snow	Shovelling cocaine
Bennett	Levèsque
CBC radio dramas	Nightclubs
Ralph Klein	Calvin Klein
Jack Gallagher	The federal deficit
Wheat	Bagels
Burton Cummings	Pierre Burton
Minor league hockey	The Maple Leafs
The Calgary Sun	*The Toronto Sun*
Cow pies	Quiche
Alberta separatists	Quebec separatists
Pancake breakfasts	Brunch
Prairie oysters	Oysters

WHY CRIME DIFFERS IN THE EAST
IT'S ORGANIZED
by Nicholas Pashley

Let us begin by noting that crime is not the same in the East and the West. To begin with, crime in the East is more, shall we say, organized. Popular crimes in the West have always been drunk and disorderly conduct, drunk driving, drunk ploughing, drunk walking, refusal to undergo breathalyzer testing, cattle rustling, and cattle rustling while under the influence. While Westerners are certainly capable of planning to get drunk, their crimes tend to be impetuous acts, born of the desperation of living in Didsbury, Alberta.

The Easterner, by contrast, might have a drink, but when it comes to crime he is alert, efficient, and sober. The eastern criminal is not a hobbyist. Contrary to the old adage, one can make a good buck out of crime if one is prepared to put in the long hours and dedication necessary.

It is important, first of all, to identify the crime that is right for you. A highly skilled jewel thief, for instance, might turn out to be a washout as a pimp, forger, or cabinet minister. Unfortunately, the law allows you only so much trial and error in these matters, so you'll have to settle on your particular line of crime early on.

Practical considerations aside, crime in eastern Canada has its local biases. In Montreal, for instance, robbing banks has long been a regional speciality. Outlaws in Toronto, on the other hand, habitually face charges

like trying to procure a drink after one a.m., attempting to dine without a reservation, and wearing brown shoes with a blue suit.

Motorcycle enthusiasts seeking new business opportunities.

Over the years, mayors and police chiefs have told Torontonians that Organized Crime — as opposed to organized crime — does not exist in that fair city. (For the beginner, Organized Crime is much like organized crime except that one commits the former with people one is related to, or with an organization with a name that makes no sense to outsiders — Cosa Nostra, for example, or Mulroney Caucus.)

Ottawa, of course, is rife with Organized Crime. Innocent citizens are misled, defrauded, and robbed on a daily basis, and most of them don't even live there. And the worst part is that nobody pays even lip service to the notion of stopping these vile practices. Even in Montreal the forces of respectability make occasional threats to interfere with the livelihood of the malefactors who prey on the innocent, but in Ottawa the worst of the wrongdoers get armed protection from their victims.

A similar situation exists in the Atlantic provinces. In New Brunswick, to cite an example, there is a Mr. Big figure called R*ch*rd H*tf**ld. Known

to those around him as Disco Dick or Da Premier. H*tf**ld's name has been connected with drugs, the corruption of youth, and failing to lower the unemployment rate. Yet H*tf**ld remains a free man. And so it is with New Brunswick's *Grand Fromage*. Yet there are signs of discontent even there. Members of the infamous Tory Mob, of which H*tf**ld has been the unchallenged don for more than a decade and a half, have recently been questioning the old man's leadership, and it is not unthinkable that a change might be in the works. Sensing weakness in the Tories, a rival local gang — dubbed the Liberal Party of New Brunswick — has been developing its own areas of strength in the backstreets of Saint John, preparing for an opportunity to seize control of the province's traditional crime strongholds.

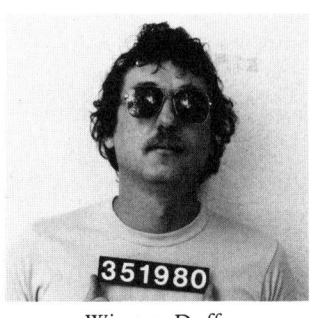

Winston Duffy
Charged with Bill 101 infraction by Language Police. Was caught serving carp (instead of carpe). Currently serving 2-5.

The underworld in Newfoundland, long operated by the legendary J**y Sm*llw**d, has in recent years come to be dominated by a single family, the much-feared Cr*sb** clan. J*hn Cr*sb**, the ambitious patriarch of the family, has made no secret in the past of his desire to expand his empire, and is said to have been narrowly defeated some few years ago by an Irish crime figure called M*lr*n*y (the exact pronunciation of whose name is known only to a few insiders) in a bid to take over the most lucrative criminal operation in the country: the federal government. Clearly, Cr*sb** is a man to be watched.

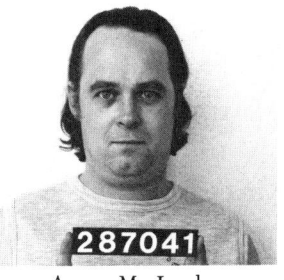

Angus MacLeod
Masterminded Frank Miller's campaign for premier. Convicted of gross negligence. Currently serving 2-end of Liberal reign.

Still, for sheer volume, variety, violence, and general charisma in organized crime, it's hard to beat the province of Quebec, and in particular the great city of Montreal. Statistics show that at one time or another virtually every Montrealer has robbed a bank. It's good clean

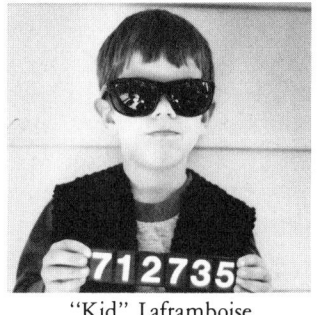

"Kid" Laframboise
Organized crime boss. Bored with traditional atrocities, recently produced his first feature film: *MEAN SESAME STREETS* starring Robert de Meany as "Big Nerd."

fun for the whole family, and the pay's not bad either. In recent years, however, the banks of Montreal have been bled dry and would-be robbers have been forced to line up and wait for a chance at the better targets. As a result, many of Montreal's better bank-job artists have been venturing farther afield, some as far as Toronto. After all, Toronto is famous for its banks, and Torontonians have traditionally had too much respect for their banks to think of robbing them, so security is less vigilant. The problem has become so intense now that Toronto banks give hiring preference to tellers who can read French hold-up notes.

It is easy to keep up with the crime scene in Montreal, at least for those with some ability to read French. While the anglophone *Gazette* makes an effort to cover the major killings and arrests, only *Le Journal de Montreal* treats the city's criminal life with the lurid respect it warrants. Daily reading of *Le Journal* can be supplemented with weekly magazines like *Allo Police* and *Photo Police*, both of which feature splendidly artistic photographs of murderers and victims, as well as auto maintenance tips and interesting ads for marital aids. *Photo Police* also carries a feature in which a photogenic and apparently uninhibited young woman assists readers with their sexual problems in prose that is both candid and engaging.

The anglophone reader can enjoy these publications with the aid of a French-English dictionary and a vivid imagination. Key words and phrases to be learned and memorized include *le meurtre, le double meurtre, la victime, l'assassin, le revolver, tuer, abbattre, violer, accuser, acquitter* (rare), and *vingt-deux coups de couteau.*

Crime in Quebec, unlike government, is highly organized. And when we say organized, we mean Organized. In Montreal, people lead more public lives than they do in Toronto, so they're more likely to kill each other in public, particularly in bars, discos, and the traditional Italian restaurant. Very often the parties involved are said to be "known to the police," but if the police have no idea who did it, they call it a "settling of accounts." These are the niceties that have to be observed after "a gangland slaying."

Traditional criminals of this sort no longer have a monopoly on organized crime in Quebec. In recent years they have been joined by some surprising groups of people, including a very well known club of motorcycle enthusiasts called the H*ll's *ng*ls. Now there was a time when the H*ll's *ng*ls were just a bunch of fun-seeking guys with a taste for leather and

male camaraderie, but somewhere along the line they probably discovered that if they were going to be outlaws they might as well make a buck out of it.

Like their competitors in the M*f** , the lads in leather have shown themselves remarkably adept at killing each other. In the summer of 1985, Quebec police, acting on a "tip," fished the remains of six H*ll's *ng*ls out of the St. Lawrence. As I write, a number of other motorcycle enthusiasts are — to use the charming English expression — "assisting the police with their enquiries."

Bikers seldom attend church. If they own suits, they are strictly for court appearances, which tend to be frequent. Bikers gladly call themselves outlaws, and blatantly don't give a fig for society. They are perfectly happy to sell people drugs, women, or protection. Members of the M*f**, on the other hand, are dependable Catholics, well-dressed upholders of the traditional values, who are perfectly happy to sell people drugs, women, or protection.

Speaking of protection, what about the police? Not all of the Montreal police force are corrupt. A cursory reading of the crime weeklies presents a cavalcade of policemen, half of them being decorated for acts of courage, the rest being arraigned for major offences. But then who's perfect? It wasn't a Montreal cop who made the crack about eastern bastards freezing in the dark. Montreal cops — and their counterparts in Toronto, Moncton, and St. John's — are just working stiffs who have to pay for their gas like everybody else, with no Heritage Fund to fall back on. There are no safe guidelines for the unsuspecting western visitor to follow here; just hope for the best.

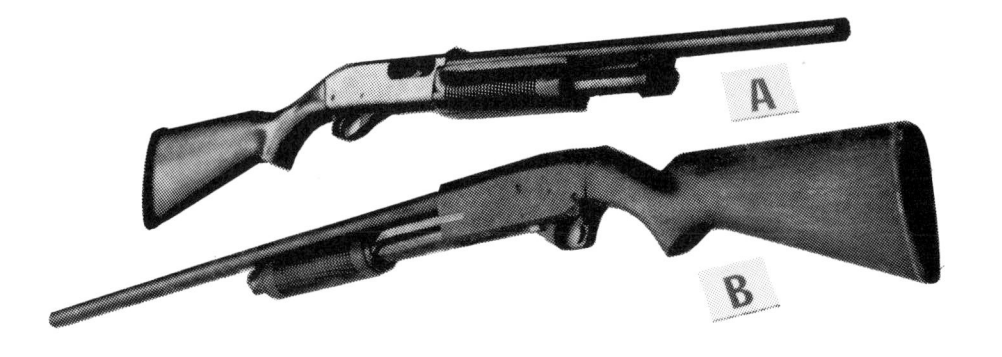

JOIN THE RECORD CLUB OF EASTERN CANADA AND GET THREE RECORDS FREE!

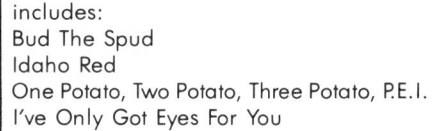

EAST IS EAST
BUT WEST IS BEST
The CFL and the NHL
by Don Gillmor

Football fans have known for some time that the West consistently produces better teams than the East. Occasionally, an eastern squad will rally as the Argos did in '83, but generally it is the West that harbours not only the Grey Cup champion but the two best teams as well.

With their names firmly emblazoned on the Stanley Cup, the Edmonton Oilers seem to be making a potent case for western hockey dominance as well. Given that there is a larger population and more money in the East (not counting the Heritage Fund), this state of affairs seems unnatural. How does the West produce better teams than the East? An examination of eastern and western life styles yields some clues.

Westerners are often steered towards a career in professional hockey at a very early age. The West is full of icy sidewalks, farm machinery and snowballs with rocks in them, with the result that few reach adolescence with all their teeth.

"It's the rink for you, Seth, you can't be runnin' the feed store with that godawful smile a yours."

Easterners may chip a tooth when their fettucine arrives a little too *al dente*, but the result is usually a lawsuit rather than a hockey career.

The glowing exception to eastern hockey inferiority is Quebec, where hockey still runs neck and neck with armed robbery as the route to

Outremont, though lately it seems the latter profession has been attracting the cream of that province's toothless youth.

Toronto has only produced one skater of distinction—Toller Cranston. Drafted by the Maple Leafs in '79, he provided a stylish defense, taking his man through a scintillating *pas de deux* that often culminated in a triple axel jump. Offensively, however, he failed to provide the punch the Leafs needed, and he was released later that year following a dispute with management over dressing room decor.

Western youths, fired in the kiln of harsh prairie winters and forbidding distances, are more attuned to the general concept of ice and are prepared to fight at the drop of a puck, two qualities necessary for a pro career. The eastern understanding of ice doesn't go much past its role in a campari and soda, and Easterners are more apt to consult a lawyer than fight. In the West, through the nine winter months in the West there is little other than hockey and the CBC for entertainment. By the time a Westerner reaches the age of fifteen, he knows more about hockey than Don Cherry and wouldn't know Mary Lou Finlay if she fell out of a grain bin.

Another advantage the West has on the professional level is that their fans want winning teams. Maple Leaf fans will watch anything and have been known to give the Zamboni driver a standing ovation. Montrealers enjoy winning teams to the extent that they cheer for whoever is winning, whether it's the Canadiens or the Pittsburgh Penguins. They insist on being on the winning side and are more adaptable than Durum wheat when it comes to loyalties. Nordique fans like to see Quebec beat Montreal, but would just as soon bomb the legislature as witness a win against New Jersey or L.A.

The situation as it exists in football is more readily perceived because of the frank delineation between East and West.

On the whole, for much of the last two decades, the West has produced superior ball clubs while the East has produced a better warm lamb and radacchio salad. Part of the difference lies in the calibre of available local talent, usually culled from university football programs and junior football associations. In Saskatchewan, a Roughrider scout need only tour the section roads until he finds two hulking brothers carrying their John Deere out to the field in an effort to save gas. For a token sum and the promise

of a meeting with the reigning Miss Farm Implements, he has two interior linemen who could stop a train.

In Toronto, scouts are relegated to institutions like the George Brown College of Interior Design. Recruiting for the Concordes in Montreal is limited to combing discos for men who can do a convincingly funky end-zone dance. The chances of finding anyone who could get the ball there, however, are almost non-existent. Montrealers like their violence on the ice or with some political motivation, and so haven't warmed to football.

To come up with the western entry, the West uses a playoff system that has the second- and third-place finishers competing to play against the first-place team on its home field. While not perfect, this arrangement usually produces the squad best able to reach down into their guts and come up with the big one, so to speak.

The East has gone through a number of playoff systems in an attempt to produce a champion, rarely producing anything like one. The latest system has the coaches of the two teams that won more than four games meeting for lunch.

"Why don't you go, Bob?"

"We went last year. You go."

"Forget it. It's winter out there now."

"Well, someone has to go."

"Our fat guy who hikes the ball quit. We can't go."

"You can have our fat guy."

"You getting lunch?"

"Sure. Good luck against those mutants."

"Thanks. Ciao."

"THE AVENGING CONSCIENCE"

Two hopefuls try out for the position of wide receiver at the Argos spring training camp.

That eastern teams are a little less threatening is evidenced by the banter that goes on between linemen before the ball is snapped.

Western player: "I'm going to take your head off and spit down your neck, dickbrain."

Eastern player: "Let's do lunch some-time."

There is, of course, the dry cold. The West has a celebrated dry cold that helps to sustain life when the temperature goes below –20, the average temperature for a Grey Cup game. The damp cold that plagues the East causes no end of problems for those players who didn't know there was life north of San Diego until they were drafted by Ottawa. An outright refusal to leave their homes after October 1 often results in momentum-breaking holes in the starting roster. Yet western imports don't hesitate to play in

–22 weather at Taylor Field once they have been assured it is a dry cold.

"It's 22 below, man. I ain't playin'. I ain't leavin' the ho–tel."

"It's a dry cold, Moses."

"That be cool."

Perhaps the single greatest reason for eastern inferiority in either sport is the fact that Harold Ballard doesn't own any western teams. It has been observed by long-suffering fans of the Leafs that the primary difference between western and eastern hockey is the role of the frozen horse turd. In the West, it is used in place of a real puck, while in the East it often substitutes for a real owner. Ballard is known around Toronto as a man whose head resembles a twelve pound uncooked pot roast that harbours the thoughts of a much better cut. His plans to rebuild the Leafs stem from an indisputable logic. "Why pay good money for a few hot shots when I can bring up the entire farm team for the same price? I can ship half of St. Catherines here for what I'm paying that Swedish meatball."

Ballard has an equally deft touch with his football team, the Hamilton Tiger-Cats. "Anyone who comes to see these overpaid bums is a fool," he announced in an effort to erode a once formidable base of fan support. The daring ploy worked, and by season's end discounted Ti-Cat tickets made available to the few remaining Stelco workers couldn't be given away. One of the CFL rule changes being considered for the next season stipulates that for every eastern team Ballard owns he must own at least one western squad. If there is every to be any parity in the CFL, this is a critical first step.

However, should the West ever want to engage us in a brunching competition, lobster-eating contest, or a maple sugaring-off, they will find themselves in the battle of their lives.

THE EASTERN TRIVIA QUIZ

1) Montreal hosts the world's biggest:
   a. exodus
   b. pothole
   c. bomb squad
   d. jazz festival
   e. crime festival

2) The primary export of Cabbagetown is:
   a. cabbages
   b. the working class
   c. heterosexuals
   d. Shawn O'Sullivan

3) Quebec's biggest industry is:
   a. maple syrup
   b. packing up and moving to Toronto
   c. stripping in bars owned by Greeks
   d. graft

4) After the election, Brian Mulroney immediately renovated:
   a. his election promises
   b. 24 Sussex Drive
   c. Tammany Hall
   d. his image as a chain-smoking booze artist

5) Richard Hatfield is the author of:
   a. "Packing Tips for a Royal Tour"
   b. his own demise

   c. "Don't be Fooled by Oregano"
   d. "The Taxpayers' Guide to Montreal"

6) Toronto recently won the national championship in what sport?
   a. the white-wine toss
   b. power brunching
   c. raspberry duck hunting (nouvelle division)
   d. the two-man Beaujolais trials

7) Solomon Gundy is:
   a. a Jewish tailor
   b. a suspect maritime delicacy
   c. a suspect maritime politician
   d. The King of Halifax

8) McClelland and Stewart is to Canadian publishing what:
   a. Pierre Berton is to nude wrestling
   b. Farley Mowat is to Armani's spring line
   c. Margaret Atwood is to long-haul trucking
   c. Leonard Cohen is to light comedy

9) Toronto's Tiny Perfect Mayor was:
   a. Sleepie
   b. Grumpie
   c. Dopie
   d. Crombie

10) Newfoundland was the last province to join:
   a. the twentieth century
   b. Confederation
   c. a brother and sister in matrimony

11) Finish this Montreal summertime phrase; "It's not the heat, it's the:"
   a. Expos
   b. humidity
   c. arson
   d. lack of downtown parking

12) Jean Drapeau has been called:
   a. the father of Expo '67
   b. the mother of Olympic debt
   c. the godfather of Soul

13) Newfoundland has Canada's largest deposits of:
   a. resentment
   b. Newfie jokes
   c. undiscovered talent
   d. flipper pie

14) When Ottawa is looking for a good time it goes:
   a. bowling
   b. to Hull
   c. to a travel agent

15) Quebec City is the historic site of:
   a. weekly hockey violence
   b. Jacques Cartier's landing
   c. continued animosity

16) The Ontario Censorship Board refused to allow what film to be shown in that province?
   a. *Virgin on the Verge*
   b. *Thigh Noon*
   c. *Inky the Reluctant Crow*
   d. *The Tin Drum*

ALBERTA'S OIL BOOM
An Eastern Perspective
by Sarah Gardner

Prior to 1972, not much was booming in the East other than babies. News arrived one day that Cadillac dealerships in Calgary couldn't keep cars on the lot due to the demand from recent oil millionaires. This rumor precipitated a chapter of eastern history that saw one third of the eastern population move West within a year. When the going got tough, the tough moved to Alberta.

Those who stayed East knew that Alberta boasted a view of the mountains and more than their share of both cows and winters but little else. Information began to trickle in; they were paying twelve dollars an hour for pipeline workers. With overtime you could clear eight thousand a month. Applicants needed only a pair of steel-toed boots and the ability to stand around on the tundra and roll joints. Accommodation was cheap and abundant, and western women were open to suggestion, largely due to the magic of horseback riding.

There was, rumour had it, a sign at the Saskatchewan/Alberta border that read; "Last one to leave, please turn out the lights." Even Westerners were going West.

As more rumors surfaced, a profile emerged. There were more big dreams, big drinks, fast money, firm handshakes, good jobs, half-tons, lizard skin boots and unbridled optimism in Calgary than anyplace you cared to name. If you spoke English, could multiply and had two hundred dollars to invest, you were millionaire material.

In the eastern papers they advertised for geologists, engineers, interior designers who could work with wagon wheels, and cocktail waitresses who didn't mind being addressed as "Little Lady." All positions paid exorbitantly and allegedly included reliable tips on leaked wellsite tests, new strikes and development deals. Perennial home to the Largest Outdoor Show on Earth, sixteen-ounce T-bones and barrel racers named Honey, it was now host to a growing pile of petro dollars. Postcards from the first wave of opportunists arrived with a hurried scrawl: "Real estate is tripling every half hour."

Not all Easterners jumped on the band wagon. Grim-faced Ontario farmers who raised tobacco and antiques issued a biblical warning, "Greed, sin and corruption. Whole province headed for damnation."

There was a large eastern sect who was of the opinion that living west of the Humber River was damnation. They had nothing but contempt for western fortunes, which they deemed of a size that invited vulgarity. "This oil money, it's terribly *recent*, isn't it?" they assured one another. Recent or otherwise, there was still the problem of what one could buy out there

with the nearest St. Laurent Boutique two thousand miles away. You could buy land, which was suitably expensive though not something you'd want to be seen with. People who were actually involved with land were either gardeners on some level or mistaken for them. The eastern aristocracy had little incentive then to join the exodus, preferring that superior indifference to their crumbling fortunes that the British have perfected.

Occasionally, one of these families would send their son West to make a man of him. Drawing on his connections and an education that perhaps leaned a bit too heavily toward managing inherited wealth, he obtained a job as financial linchpin in a growing oil company. Failing spectacularly at making venture capital do something other than vanish, he legged it home, returning with little other than a taste for bowlegged women and a tendency to whoop. The idea of Calgary as a sort of India where you sent your milksop to be converted into officer material plainly wasn't working out.

These young men were reintroduced into the polite society of Ontario politics or family business, where employers weren't such sticklers for results. They related their western experience in tones of guarded optimism, "There's still money in the streets out there. But the catch is you have to be smart now."

But in the Toronto spirit of adventure that has given us lite beer for seven innings at Exhibition Stadium, we cautiously pressed on. It was decided to send the criminal element out West to test the waters. Some of us felt frankly that it could be a trap. As soon as they got everyone out there they were going to put them into work camps and take over the federal government.

The Alberta news became grim. A co-worker's brother-in-law described the events in a letter from the front lines. It seems that one night while the whole province was sleeping through another Jack Daniels and cocaine fog, the economy collapsed like last year's lawn furniture. When Albertans woke up the next morning looking for their Tony Lama genuine sea turtle cowboy boots, they found that someone had fallen asleep at the economic switch. The ranch-style split level with intercom in every room that had been purchased yesterday for two hundred and ten thousand dollars was now worth forty-two five, tops.

CRANSTON
BLYTHINGTON & WHELK

Some of the nouveau Westerners began to return home, pale, shaking and incoherent,"4 bdrm . . . 3 appl . . . modern eat-in kit . . 79 BMW fac. air, immac, extrs . . . must see, best offer." Most returnees were capable of speaking only in classified ad abbreviations at first. When the message was decoded we discovered they'd lost the whole shooting match. Once they were safely immersed in speech therapy and government welfare programs, a sad tale unfolded from the survivors.

The price of gas had dropped due to a glutted market, the fields were drying up and the Arabs (working with Quebec) were behind the whole thing. Albertans remembered that the Lougheed government had promised to use the oil revenue to diversify, thereby insuring a future free of the vagaries of the oil market. "We forgot." came the official word from Edmonton, extinguishing all hope.

We learned from the first wave of returnees that oil executives were leaping out of windows faster than you could say Jack Gallagher. Everyone had lost at least one friend to falling oilmen. "Squashed like a bug on the sidewalk of life by a Gulf VP" they explained in their adopted colloquialisms.

Third-hand we got the solemn statistics: there were more widows, orphans, unsold cowboy boots, unleased office space, divorces, defaulted mortgages, foreclosures, suicides, alcoholics, abandoned wives, ill winds, used trucks, manic depressives, cancelled George Jones concerts, and alien cattle mutilators per square foot in Alberta than anywhere on God's green earth.

The eastern papers reported that the only people who had bothered to keep savings accounts were paperboys and six-year-olds who had gotten a dollar on their birthday every year. Everyone else had used their money as a down payment for something that was going to double in value the next week, which was pretty well everything except tickets to a Trudeau fund-raising dinner.

We were informed by *The Toronto Sun* that on the morning of the collapse everyone had tried to unload their investments through the classified ads in the *Calgary Herald*. That historic edition was apparently six hundred and twenty-two pages, weighed twelve pounds and signalled the plummeting of every market not directly related to rye whiskey. "Homes for Sale" often included the two cars in the driveway, ten rooms of furniture and a three-year-old dressed as Buffalo Bill.

The rest of the eastern element began to limp home, filling the Number One highway with rhinestone cowboys in pearl-buttoned shirts and string ties. Dressed in the native costume of their adopted province they returned to the smugness of those who had opted for the security of their clerical position with Cranston, Blythington and Whelk.

Many returnees have been assimilated into eastern society, but occasionally a voice can be overheard in a Yorkville restaurant, "Gimme one of your 24-oz. T-bones, Honey, with a shot of red eye whiskey . . . and a beer for my horse."

FLORIDA
Canada's Eleventh Province
by Patrick Cotter

Western Canadians know Easterners are weak little things barely able to survive the mild winters east of Winnipeg, while intrepid Westerners heroically endure the frozen black despair of the Prairies. What they don't know is that these clever Easterners annually scuttle by the hundreds of thousands to the eleventh and southernmost province (Florida) to escape the central fact of Canadian life: the cold.

Despite the devalued dollar and the dangers of living in a free country where guns can be bought along with groceries, these refugees from the freezing north are thriving. Canadians are as much a part of the Sunshine State as rednecks, retirees and bona fide refugees from Cuba, Haiti and the

dying industrial cities of the northern U.S. In some of Miami's northern suburbs and large parts of Fort Lauderdale, Canadians have completely taken over, much to the dismay of local restaurateurs who watch their best tables tied up for hours by soft-drink sipping sons and daughters of Confederation to whom a tip is a piece of free advice.

Canadians new to Florida should discreetly disguise their origins. Wearing socks with sandals is a sure tip-off. Avoid flaunting your nationality. Flashing a little green will get you a lot farther. Remember, this is Sunbelt America and Florida is state-of-the-art America when it comes to subdivide and conquer. Most of the senior citizens in Florida are older than the vast majority of the flimsy buildings and shoddy homes. Think of it as the last frontier, with settlers arriving in station wagons instead of covered wagons.

Besides throwing up developments faster than hurricanes can knock them down and squeezing oranges and tourists, counting drug money is another booming industry. While Florida welcomes anyone with a dollar to spend, some things don't cost a cent: You can watch a space shuttle launch or rub elbows with a shark.

But most Canadians go to Florida simply to get warm. Here are some words of warning: 1. Most psychiatrists agree that you should stay home if you have a bad reaction to malls, plazas and shopping centers. 2. Keep your political opinions to yourself. Trying to deduce a Floridian's views and his threshold for erupting into violence merely from his appearance is much like picking mushrooms on a random basis and hoping they're not poisonous. 3. Avoid getting sick. Provincial governments are not very interested in footing the bill for Canadians who fall ill on vacation. American health-care costs will quickly convince you to wait until you get home to seek treatment, unless of course you have severed a limb or discovered that your heart is no longer beating.

Florida may look the same from top to bottom to the first time visitor, but differences do exist. Key West might now be more accurately called Gay West. Papa Hemingway would be furious at what they've done to his beloved town. The once sleepy fishing village looks as though it has been done over by an army of interior decorators.

Miami is the Montreal of the U.S. as far as biculturalism is concerned. If Spanish sounds like gibberish to you, steer clear. Unofficially, English has

become the second language in the sprawling city inextricably linked with vice. Fort Lauderdale, most famous for its Spring Break wet T-shirt contests and rampaging college kids, has become a sprawling suburb of Miami.

The rest of the east coast is a string of seaside towns distinguishable in name only, broken by the Daytona Speedway.

The rest of the state is composed of swamp, enormous cattle ranches, orange groves, golf courses, military bases, university towns, a state capital, Disney World, water theme parks and 623 roadside attractions featuring alligators sleeping in stagnant green water.

Westerners should not construe the East's stranglehold on Florida as just another instance of a feast for the East and the rest for the West. There is plenty of room left on the world's largest sandbar. Maybe I can interest you in a few choice oceanfront acres where the balmy sea breezes never end?

YOU ARE ABOUT TO ENTER
THE WESTERN SECTOR